C. CHASE CAREY MBA

CHASIN' MEDITATION

THE STEP BY STEP GUIDE TO A STRESS-FREE LIFE THROUGH MEDITATION

Chasin' Meditation
By C. Chase Carey MBA

Publishing Support Provided by:
XXXXXXX

ISBN: 0615980600
ISBN 13: 9780615980607
Library of Congress Control Number: 2014904450
Accelerated Change Concepts, Inc., Alpharetta, GA

Printed in the United States of America

Chasin' Meditation is dedicated to my daughter,

Kaitlin T. Carey

PERCEPTION VS. REALITY

Do You Have to Be a Yogi Sitting on a Rock for 50 Years in
Order to Know How to Meditate?

Or

Can *Normal* People, Like You and Me,
Learn to Meditate Too?

Which One is True For <u>You</u>?

You **Can** Learn to Meditate and **Will** Be in About 90 Minutes.....

(Applause!)

ACKNOWLEDGEMENTS

There are many people I would like to thank for helping me to create this, my first book on Meditation. My goal, and that of the people who support me, is to teach millions of people how to use Meditation to improve their lives. Particularly using it to understand and release the stress in their lives forever. And I mean, *forever*. There are some wonderful people who chose to help me but asked that their names remain private. Their contributions were just as important as of those mentioned here, and I am grateful for their help.

My Wife, Lisa Carey. Lisa "Las Vegas" Carey, is first and foremost. 13 years ago I left the corporate world, a comfortable paycheck, and a 401(K) and had to start all over. Impossible at my age, many said. Improbable with my health challenges, I knew. But not once, ever, did Lisa leave my side. Not once did she stop believing in my dreams, perhaps at times believing in them more strongly than I.

Dr. Catherine P. Perry. An important double mention for Dr. Perry. Not only did her Reiki and Intuitive Healing move me beyond sickness, but she also Peer-Reviewed the book and presented invaluable additional information and insight. The book would not be nearly as effective as it is without her critical input and desire to see it successful.

People from all walks of life trust Dr. Perry's wisdom and healing abilities to help them unlock the doors to their happiness, greater health, financial prosperity, harmonious relationships, and peace-of-mind (www.CatherinePPerry.com). Dr. Perry is one of the first professionals to give Reiki treatments at a major US corporation (thank you, Johnson & Johnson Pharmaceuticals), and is looking for an even greater level of Corporate partnership. Please learn about her. She is an intuitive spiritual healer, inspirational speaker, psychologically oriented spiritual life coach, and author of the empowering, award-winning book, Courageous Wake.

Harvey Grady, Center for Human Potential. A remarkable man with a remarkable story with remarkable talents and a remarkable drive to teach people how to improve their own lives.

My Writing Partner, Cathryn Marshall. We spent many productive hours writing together, she on her book, Simple Fat Burn, and me on *Chasin' Meditation*. Together we brainstormed, wordsmithed, wrote and rewrote our books, figuring out how to best help people, how to best present ideas, and how to dive in and write like we never had to stop.

My Board of Advisors. People of unbelievable talent and success, willing to chip in, asking only to help, not to be paid. My Leadership Panel, in alphabetical order: Peg Eitl, Ramez Helou, Bryan Karetny, Karen Malik, Sarah McLean, Tamara O'Neill, and Dr. Catherine P. Perry, M.Ed, DD; At Large Advisors are, again in alphabetical order: Andre Coman, Dr. Aaron Fausz, Ph.D, Render Freeman, Esq., Jennifer Heal, Cathryn (Cat) Marshall, Margaret Mills, Jeffrey Shumaker, and Jeanna ("Gina") Zelin. An additional very special thank you to Sarah McLean, for bringing me back "home" (wink).

A very special thanks to Katheryn Small of Profound Impact for her keen visionary insight and for naming *Chasin' Meditation* so brilliantly.

Also, in alphabetical order: Dawn Andrews, Rick Bailey, Georgi Baldwin, Mr. Mark Burns, Becca Bonacchi, Alice Fink, Seema Jani, Rob Mello, Elaine Mueller, RN, HN-BC, Dorothy Thomas, Jeff Tormey, and Elizabeth C. Vevera, MD..

Sarah McLean's Inaugural Class of SEED Meditation® Teachers, who taught me more than I ever imagined possible in 6 work-intensive days: Robin Byrne, Suzanne Campbell, Avianna Castro, Joyce Duchscherer, Liz Garlieb, Jules Green, Darlene Hamilton, Pamela Joy, Lynn Carriere Lessard, Margaret Mills, Marsha Nieland, Angela Sands, Sonja Schramm, Carol Studenka, Birgit Walker, and Missy Wooten. Gifted beings who can also teach you the wonderful world of Meditation. You can learn more about them at http://www.sedonameditation.com/meditation-teachers.htm

Photographer Modesto Orizzonte. Special thanks to Modesto Orizzonte of Modest Eyes Photography (www.pbase.com/orizzonte), for the use of his photo of Katheryn Small on the Perception vs. Reality page.

Ms. Aubrey Jordan Burns, for her "Flower Child" photo on page 108.

And to my Editors, Rosemary Dreger, Jacki Flynn, and Beth Hermes who took my ideas and experiences and made them so understandable!

All photos not listed above are licensed from Fotolia.com.

TABLE OF CONTENTS

"You will begin to Meditate when you are ready to meet the real you."

~ C. Chase Carey, MBA

HOW TO READ THIS BOOK

Welcome. Whether you are new to Meditating, sort of got started once, or Meditated regularly years ago and now want to get back into it, I promise you fun, wonderment, and a lot less *Stress* in your life.

What Kind of Meditation Do I Teach?

The first question many people ask me is, "What kind of Meditation do you teach?" My answer is that I *primarily* teach three forms of Meditation, each of which is Guided or uses Guided Imagery:

1. The first form is a simple, straightforward form of Meditation which can be used for Stress release and many other things. It is Sarah McLean's Simple Easy Every Day (SEED) Meditation™ Method. Although it is not specifically taught in this book it can be learned in workshops throughout the US. (For more information on the SEED Meditation® Method, see www.sedonameditation.com/meditationteachers.htm).

2. The second form I teach uses the Stress Domino, which will allow you to more fully and more quickly understand all the pieces of Stress and, therefore, more fully and more immediately release your stress - permanently.

3. The third form I teach is the Inner Essence Meditation™ which I also refer to as a Global Access Meditation Method. This topic is detailed in Chapter 9, which by the way, contains 98% of the information in the book. IE Meditation teaches people to dialogue with their Inner Essences and High Essence (aka higher guidance), establish a relationship, and engage in that relationship to accelerate the release Stress and to solve problems, whether the problems are in their personal life, business life, spiritual life, or to simply satisfy their innate curiosity. **Inner Essence Meditation is a Deep Dive, advanced form of Meditation which greatly accelerates your access to places and results that normally would take much longer to achieve. IE Meditation gives you direct access to your Inner Intelligence.**

When you use accelerating forms of Meditation to make changes in your life, like a recalcitrant child, you may get internal "push back," which manifests itself in external disruption, but along with the fuss comes better and faster changes. With Inner Essence Meditation™ you can achieve many of these results, greatly accelerated over more traditional forms of Meditation:

- Stress Elimination
- Problem Solving in Business
- Problem Solving in Life
- Trauma and Grief Release
- Memory Improvement
- Life Planning
- Choice Analysis
- Connection with Higher Consciousness
- And about 10,000 additional, even more fascinating things

So even though I categorize Inner Essence Meditation™ as the third kind of Meditation, it is truly a **Global Access Meditation Method from which all desires and outcomes from all other Meditations can be achieved.**

> Key Note: Inner Essence Meditation™ is truly a *Global Access Meditation Method* from which all desires and outcomes used in all other Meditations can be achieved.

There are other forms and techniques of Meditation I use, as well. They use Visualization and Guided Imagery.

Most all Meditation I teach is Guided, which means I, or someone else, guides you into, through, and out of your Meditations. Meditation, once learned, does not require external guidance, but it can be extremely helpful to both the new and experienced Meditator.

The Inner Essence Meditation uses Guided Imagery, which is Guided Meditation + Visualization. See Chapter 9 for more on the IE Meditation.

Please don't get hung up on all these forms, methods, and techniques. Simply learn to Meditate gently, as often as you can, working up to daily. Most of the book details this kind of Meditating. It will take you through all this bit by bit.

This book is set up into 3 Sections plus an Appendix:

Part One – Meditation

Part Two – REMOVING Stress (aka Stress No More!)

Part Three – Deep Dive / Advanced Meditation Techniques Using Inner Essences to Eliminate Stress and Emotional Blocks Immediately and Permanently.

The Appendix

In Part One you will get a good, solid, concise introduction to Meditation, what it is and isn't, what to do and what not to do, and then you will be walked through an actual Meditation.

Part Two will teach you the Stress Domino, tying all the hidden aspects of Stress together, and then walk you through a Meditation using the Domino to permanently remove your stressors.

Part Three introduces Inner Essences and their counterparts. This is an accelerating, Deep Dive, Advanced form of Meditation that is used to gain faster and longer lasting insight to the challenges you face in any and every aspect of your life. It will accelerate desired changes in your life.

By the way, the book can be read in two ways:

- Parts One, Two, and then do Meditations in the Appendix, return to Part Three, then run Meditations in the Appendix again, or

- Parts One, Two, Three, and then do Meditations in the Appendix.

You can wait on Part Three until you have some practice under your belt without missing any of the benefits of the first two parts of the book. Return to Part Three at any time when you are ready for a Deeper Dive.

The Appendix will give you a basketful of Meditations to be used for many common challenges and misconceptions abundant in modern life.

Meditation is a tool for **you** to use to improve **your** life and to explore **your** universe, without needing a space suit. Please send post cards of your travels!

The most important thing I can teach you about Meditation is that it is not what happens to you IN Meditation, but what happens OUTSIDE of Meditation in your external life that counts.

The vast majority of all Meditations are quiet and sometimes mildly informative. Think of Meditating as going to the gym for your mind and emotion. What you do in the gym is rather routine and not too exciting. But what you can do when you leave the gym is a world apart from what you could do before you went into the gym.

Last thing. I end each chapter with Three Things to Know. The same 3 Things each time. Why? I want each of you to really know and accept them into your way of life.

"I know a lot of successful people, and they all Meditate"
~ Mia Hannah, Realtor, Atlanta, GA

Almost *everybody* is <u>already</u> -
ALMOST - *Meditating!*

You Are Probably One of Them.

(...and if not, you will be in about 90 minutes!)

PART ONE - MEDITATION

Okay, it's not exactly this.......but this is not a bad start.

CHAPTER ONE

WHAT IS MEDITATION?

*"When you are ready to meet the true you, you
will begin to Meditate."*
~ *C. Chase Carey, MBA*

The phrase above is something I like to share with my students who may not be sure they are ready to Meditate.....just yet. That's fine. There is no hurry and there is no prescribed best time. The best time is when you, the wonderful person that you are, decides it is time.

Meditation in the Western world is a serious discipline and practice with serious science behind it. Don't mistake it for something less just because you don't sweat or overload your brain during Meditation. Don't mistake it for something less because the relative percentage of people who do it is very small. Don't mistake it for something less because it is often challenging to quantify all the benefits it brings to you.

The very smartest and the most successful people of all in any aspect of life Meditate; not all, but most. Remember that these type of people rarely demonstrate the same behaviors of the struggling masses. That should speak to you. It certainly does to me.

WHAT MEDITATION IS

Meditation is being in an Expanded State of Awareness with a quieted mind and body.

We quiet the mind and body through physical and mental exercises. More will be discussed on these techniques in a couple of chapters but let me start by helping you to understand how doing this will benefit you. Because that's really what Meditation is all about and why we do it. It's not what Meditation is or isn't, or how we do or don't do it, or what does or doesn't happen in Meditation. We Meditate to change our external world, meaning Meditation is all about what happens *outside* of Meditation. It's how will it improve your life? This is exactly why I started meditating over 20 years ago. I had challenges in my life for which traditional methods did not work. I wanted my external life to be better and I was willing to do anything. Lucky me, I found out about Meditation.

WHAT REALLY HAPPENS WHEN YOU MEDITATE

Have you ever seen a house or building that was 250 or 300 years old? If you've been around the world you certainly have, and if you've been in the Northeast US and Southwest, you have, too.

Think about what a 250 or 300 year old house or building looks like today. Over the several hundred years people have painted over the stone, built wood walls over the brick, plastered, added wall board, added porches, changed roof lines and put in new windows. Not bad. The house or building could be quite nice. But have you noticed that more and more new owners are removing

4

all the built-up structures, paints, and other "improvements" to restore the building to the way the architect intended?

The same is true with us. We start life with a beautiful blueprint given to us by Nature. As we start to experience life learning from our parents, religious leaders, political leaders, teachers, neighbors, television, the web, and friends, we build upon our natural blueprint. So much so, we become people trying to live our lives based on someone else's view of what is best for us. And truthfully, that doesn't always work so well.

Meditation pierces all these built-up structures we have placed upon ourselves and takes us right back to our natural blueprint. It's there, it always has been. Just waiting for us to call upon it, once more, as we did as children. Playing in the yard with no shoes and no expectations except that we *knew* magic could and did exist at every turn.

Once you are back at Nature's blueprint, structure-free, you can re-launch whatever you wish to do in life, from what is truly who Nature intended you to be. Once you have reacquainted yourself "there," at your natural blueprint, you will stop <u>doing</u> and you will start <u>being</u>. And guess what? The biggest difference between doing and being is that being has no performance anxiety attached to it.

> Key Note: Once you are back at Nature's blueprint, structure-free, you can re-launch whatever you wish to do in life, from what is truly who Nature intended you to be. Nature never intended you to live someone else's life through your body. (If it did, it would have put somebody else in there).

Bucket List No More – aka, Don't Wait For The End of Your Life to Experience Life

When you "are" you (meaning you are "being" rather than "doing"), you will not have a bucket list. You will no longer put off "you." You will come first and you will change your understanding of life from one where you have to do all these things other people tell you to do (going to work, going to the store, not going to too many movies or too many vacations) and then, at the very, very end of your productive life, right before your health and mind fails, you will go experience a dozen really wonderful things you wanted to do all along, but which other people led you to believe were silly, or even stupid.

But it's good to wait until you're 65, 75, or 85 to do your bucket list, right? After all, your bucket list will have taken a couple of months to complete and then you'd have a couple more weeks to reflect back on them and enjoy those experiences while you can still think clearly. Then 2 weeks after you get back from your bucket spree, your bowels will have given out and your body will have quit. You won't be able to see, hear, feel or recognize anyone you know. Waiting until you are old to run through your bucket list means you would have enjoyed approximately 2 weeks of it, and then, poop! I mean poof! You're gone.

When you are "you," you will contemplate wonderful things each and every day, and you may very well start to eliminate activities that do not include wonderful or nourishing things. This couldn't possibly be bad.

You might decide to live your life as an adventure rather than as a footnote.

Key Note: When you are "you," you will contemplate wonderful things each and every day, and you may very well start to eliminate activities that do not include wonderful or nourishing things. This couldn't possibly be bad.

You might decide to life your life as an adventure rather than as a footnote.

Key Note: Do not underestimate your influence with your friends, family, neighbors, community, and in business. People will listen to you a bit more carefully and they will watch what you do with more interest once you start Meditating. They will see a *different you.*

As you become an experienced Meditator you will be excited about the benefits of Meditation, one of which is a broader understanding of life. Not all people are ready to learn about that. That is fine. You are not hear to change the masses: you are only hear to change yourself.

A real life example of why this is important is my experience Meditating on the job in the corporate world. I didn't really take 40 or 45 minutes to Meditate at work but when faced with a challenging work problem I would dim the lights, close my eyes, and while sitting in my chair, I would move into an ESA and work to problem solve. It worked great, until one day an employee walked by, looked in, looked shocked, and then beat a path away from my door. I am certain she thought I was sleeping and was going to go say something to someone. That never did seem to happen but I did realize that it might look a little odd to most people – but those days are quickly diminishing.

MEDITATION DEFINED

Remember that Meditation is being in an Expanded State of Awareness with a quieted mind and body. You are not your mind, you are not your body. So what are you? Meditation will give you the answer.

Meditation "refers to a group of techniques, such as mantra meditation, relaxation response, mindfulness meditation" and others, as quoted from the National Institute of Health, Center for Complementary and Alternative Medicine website. Hundreds of millions of people throughout the world use Meditation as a daily or regular practice to eliminate stress and to be "more connected."

You may have heard of many different types of Meditation: breath work, sound mantras, silent mantras, use of symbols, guided, non-guided, physical, and other. These are not all purely Types of Meditation as much as they are Techniques to get a person into a Meditative State. It gets a little fuzzy here, but different Types of Meditation are mostly Meditations with different *Goals*. And some are Ways to Meditate.

> Key Note: Different Types of Meditation are mostly Meditations with different *Goals*.

The origins of Meditation commonly used today have their source in Eastern cultures, including India. In the East and West, Meditation is often used in Spiritual or Religious practices. Meditation can be quite effective in both uses but can also be used simply to improve mental, emotional, and physical health, without being part of a religious practice.

We will use Meditation, in its purest and simplest state, to eliminate Stress from your life and to increase your ability to be creative, solve problems, and explore new possibilities. We will not use any religious techniques here as I want Meditation to augment your life skills, not to change your beliefs and traditions. Beliefs and traditions are wonderful aspects of people's lives, and Meditation respects your practices.

A WORD ABOUT YOGA AND MEDITATION

I am often asked if Meditation is Yoga. The answer is not exactly but that Meditation *is* a part of Yoga. The word Yoga comes from Sanskrit and means yoke or union. It is a practice that enables a person's physical, mental, and emotional bodies to be in alignment with the divine or with nature, depending on your constructs. This is a pretty big "job" so to speak, so Yoga has 8 "limbs" to it (as defined in *The Yoga Sutras of Pantanjali*, p56):

1. Yama : Laws of life
2. Niyama : Rules for Living
3. **Asanas : Body postures**
4. **Pranayama : Breathing exercises**
5. Pratyahara : Retirement of the senses
6. Dharana : Focusing of attention
7. Dhyana : Meditation
8. Samadhi : The Settled mind

In the United States, much of the Yoga practiced is #3 and a little of # 4. So when most people in the US talk about Yoga, they are really speaking about Yoga Asanas. Most people in the US are not speaking of all 8 steps when speaking of Yoga and almost always are not speaking about #7, Dhyana, which is a critical limb of Yoga.

"Yoga is the settling of the mind into silence," so Pantanjali tells us in his second Sutra. It is also my favorite definition of Yoga and why I am always excited to have Yoga practitioners in class. They have a great foundation in understanding of our alignment with unity.

LET'S LEARN A BIT MORE ABOUT MEDITATION

What Meditation Isn't

Let's look what Meditation is not. That can often help with understanding what is distinct about Meditation. Meditation is not......

- Just relaxing your body
- Just quieting your mind
- Just asking for help

Many people will share that they already Meditate. They will say they Meditate when they are…

- Gardening
- Running, riding a bike, doing vigorous exercise
- Reading

- Sitting quietly
- Doing hobbies that involve intricate work (e.g., small models, painting, etc.)
- Flying a plane
- Scuba diving
- And many, many more

All of these things encompass the first 2 steps of Meditation, but they fall just a bit short, albeit a very important bit, from Meditating. However, such people are often natural Meditation students. This is what I mean when I say, "Almost everybody is, almost, *already* Meditating."

So why are these people often natural students of Meditation? Because they are more than half-way there and they are disciplined at focus, even though sometimes the focus is light and easy.

If you do not have any such activities, Meditation will be a great start for you to learn to have such discipline. It also helps if you are a person who can "get out of your head", relinquish control, and are open to thinking differently. Think you cannot do these things? No worry, I'll teach you how. Today.

A WORD ABOUT MINDFULNESS

I am often asked what the difference is between Mindfulness and Meditation. Is someone who is practicing Mindfulness, Meditating?

Mindfulness is believed to be a very important tool in becoming Enlightened. It has its roots in a Sanskrit word, smrti, which is translated as "awareness". You can be Mindful but not Meditating, but you cannot Meditate without being Mindful.

In most Western practice, Mindfulness is softly focusing your awareness on what is going on immediately around you, as you experience it, without judgment. This specifically means without thoughts of anything in your past and future, near or far. This means you cannot think about the person that just cut you off in traffic nor can you think about what you will be doing on vacation next week.

This means not looking all around, making judgments or evaluations, or supplanting your preferences on what you see. So if you are hiking in the Mesa's and mountains of Sedona, you would softly notice the color, texture, size of rocks, plants and animals, but you would not be thinking…"wouldn't it be cool if that tree were greener." Not at all something most Westerners are used to thanks to 24/7 cable and satellite TV.

We Westerners tend to "experience" life by being in it and doing something. Mindfulness is a lot less active, *but* in this soft focus and quiet mind, you will become much more a part of where you are and what you are experiencing. Consider the difference between someone going to the beach, running in and out of the waves, throwing a Frisbee around and having "fun" vs. taking a quite walk in the surf's edge. Returning home the following week, the Frisbee throwers will not recall seashells, starfish, the advancing and retreating tide, nor the reflection of the sun on the water. Surf walkers will.

DO YOU HAVE TO CHANGE RELIGIONS WHEN YOU START TO MEDITATE?

No! Absolutely not. Meditation is used in nearly, or every, form of religion practiced on Earth. Religion and religious traditions can and do provide significant presence to many, many people. Meditation can only enhance that. If your religious traditions are supporting your goals in life, by all means, keep those traditions. The Dalai Lama supports people keeping their religious traditions when they learn Meditation.

Let me twist your thoughts on this a bit and ask you: "Do you ever ask if you need to change your religion if you start to work out in a gym?" It sounds like a kind of silly question until about 30 seconds after you hear it. If working *out* doesn't mean you have to change religions, then working *in* doesn't mean you have to change religions either.

What Meditation Is

Meditation is (simply) **"relaxing your mind and body by quieting your nervous system and then being in an expanded state of awareness (ESA)."**

Key Note: Meditation is (simply) "relaxing your mind and body by quieting your nervous system and then being in an expanded state of awareness (ESA)."

Now let's consider more things about Meditation. What's this? "Wait!" you say? "Meditation has to be more than one short and simple sentence. I was expecting at least 12 paragraphs on it."

No, sorry, it really is that simple. Surprising that more people don't do it then, right? I estimate 22 million people are Meditating at any given minute of each and every day. This is amazing when you think how powerful that is. We need to *learn* to give ourselves the *time* to Meditate.

Let's go on to describe more about Meditation. That's where you'll have plenty to read along with.

APPROACHES, TYPES, AND TECHNIQUES TO MEDITATION

Approaches, Types, and Techniques to Meditate are often overlaid onto one another and used interchangeably. This results in your friend Jennifer saying, "Oh, I was taught Gratitude Meditation, you should try that." And your friend Devon says, "I learned Guided Meditation, you should do that." And Tasha saying, "Oh, I learned Mantra Meditation, that's really the best." How can you distinguish which is best?

Well, they are all best although one (or more) may work better for you today, while another may work better for you tomorrow, depending on your personality and what you want to achieve with your Meditation practice.

There are two Approaches to Meditation:

1. Passively being in an Expanded State of Awareness (ESA); or

2. Actively seeking information, having a specific goal, in an Expanded State of Awareness.

In Passive Meditation you are simply in the moment, enjoying the nurturing Expanded State of Awareness. Specific information may or may not come to you at that time, but it is not of concern because your health will improve, your mind will become clearer and your emotions more balanced. There may or may not be brief, soft contemplation used here. Being in a Passive Meditation is an *absolutely wonderful* thing to do. Passive Meditation is what 95% of most Meditators do.

In Active Meditation, which we will use here a lot, we go after specific answers, understanding, or improvement. You can reduce Stress and eliminate Fears using Passive Meditation, but it takes longer. If you have a longer time horizon, and you are cool with that, that's great. It will work perfectly for you.

If you are like many people, you want to quickly remove Stress and enjoy sooner what's beyond it. Therefore, I will teach you both Passive and Active Meditation. We will define Active Mediation here as ***"purposeful inquiry during an Expanded State of Awareness."*** We will do it using Guided Meditation as well as Guided Imagery Meditation, dialoguing with your Inner Essences – your subconscious intelligence. (Guided Imagery is a *Technique* used in Meditation that combines a story line and visualization to create a road map, taking you directly to the answers you need.) Using Inner Essences is an Advanced Meditation Technique discussed by itself in Section Three.

Why will we use Active Meditation to remove Stress? As my Taekwondo Teacher, Mr. Mark Burns, 5th Degree Black Belt, instructs: "You can take a shot in the dark and sometimes you will hit what you are after, but mostly you won't. If you look first, pick your target, and then go after it, you *will* hit what you want." (This is probably good advice for a lot of things in life, not just Meditation). By using Active forms of Meditation, we will target the exact cause and remove it.

The main difference between Active and Passive Meditation is that in Active Meditations we are seeking direct answers to specific questions *in that Meditation*. We are not just waiting for enlightenment.

> Key Note: The main difference between Active and Passive Meditation is that in Active Meditation we are seeking direct answers to specific questions *in that Meditation*. We are not just waiting for enlightenment.

There are many Types (Goals) of Meditation:

Different types of Meditation do different things for us. If we want to release stress, we may do a Stress Domino Meditation (a form of Active Meditation), or Inner Essence Meditation (a form of Active Meditation) or we may simply move into a Meditative state (a form of Passive Meditation) and relax.

There are hundreds - if not thousands - of other Types of Meditation: Gratitude, Forgiveness, Self-Love, and many, many other things, or reasons. Pick something you want to do, for example, creating a love relationship in your life. Look for a Meditation. There is bound to be one and if there isn't and you need

one, email me and I will create one for you (time permitting).

There are many Techniques (Ways) for Meditation:

You've heard of many of them: Mantra Meditation, Breath (or Breath Work Meditation), Guided Meditation, Guided Imagery Meditation, and others. I will talk about each of these so you can get a feel for them.

Mantra Meditation. Most of us have heard of Transcendental Meditation ™ or TM™. TM is a branded form of a Silent Mantra Meditation. A Mantra is a sound, set of sounds, or a meaningless word that you say over and over in your mind while you Meditate. It is used to keep your attention away from distracting thoughts. In Sanskrit, a mantra is defined as a "sacred utterance" and Some people say that only spiritual teachers can assign you a Mantra to use and that only they should. If that is a tradition of yours, then that is fine. If it is not, then you can use one of your own. It is certainly as valid. The trick to making your own is that you have to create a word, sound, or series of sounds that have absolutely no meaning to you. That's not so easy to do, although it can be done.

Here's what I do: I silently say a Mantra in my meditation as part of the SEED Meditation® Method that I teach. It's ideal to use a Mantra that has little or no meaning, one that doesn't stimulate thinking. Some you might have heard of ..... Om, One, Amen, etc. The concept is foreign to the industrialized world, but is also very, very simple. It is key not to over-think it or to analyze it.

A Mantra is used to focus our minds on a single thing when we are distracted by thoughts in Meditation. During Meditation we quiet our minds so we can be or work in an Expanded State of Awareness. Problem is, our minds were made to think. Our brains do this automatically when responding to stimuli, which in the electronicised, mechanized, TV-ised, Web-ised, advertised world happens non-stop. With each stimulus your brain starts to think, and determine what consequences or opportunities the stimuli presents. This was an extremely effective attribute when, as cave men and women, we could round a corner and face a saber-tooth tiger. We needed our brains to get us the heck out of that situation - and fast - so we didn't end up as the tiger's lunch. It's no longer likely that we will run into tigers (although I've met some people who live in areas where that can happen) but part of the brain still responds to stimuli as if it were 1,000,000 years ago. We have simply switched from a "fight or flight" thought process to a "buy or tweet" thought process. (I just made up the "buy" or "tweet"…like it?)

Scientists say we have somewhere between 10,000 and 50,000 or 60,000 thoughts a day. In an 18-hour day, that is nearly as much as one thought a second! When you go to Meditate, those thoughts are still there. Using a Mantra does not remove those thoughts, but it keeps your attention on something other than those thoughts. You will, after practice, get to the point where you can stay "thoughtless" without a Mantra, but Mantras are very effective tools for new Meditators. (In this respect, being thoughtless is a good thing).

Let's say we are in our Meditative state (more on this in Chapter 4). Using a mantra we will make up right here, "1, 1" we gently repeat, silently, "1, 1" over and over and over again. When I use it, I visualize a water wheel slowly spinning in my direction; as I visualize this, on my in-breath I say "1" and on my out-breath I say "1". Over and over and over again, calmly and easily. It is repetitive, yes, but it doesn't feel repetitive (this is hard to explain). What happens during my Mantra Meditation if I grab notice and follow one of the thoughts floating through my mind? Once I notice *that I am noticing* the stray thought, I simply and gently return to the Mantra. I don't judge myself for "slipping" and I don't worry about it. I simply return to the  Mantra. Later on, when I grab notice of another thought, I once again, gently and without judgment, return to the Mantra.

You may also know of people (often monks) who chant during Meditation, often using the word, Om. By the way, Om is believed to be the sound of creation and in my experience is an effective tool to help in Meditation. I have used chanting Om many times in a healing circle – it is very, very powerful. (I cannot explain the physiology behind it but I can testify to its significant healing effect.) I have also used Om to begin Meditation sessions. The Monroe Institute is a big believer in the use of Om to start Meditations. At "Monroe," we chant Om out loud and loudly to boot. I did feel a little silly when I first did it, but you get used to it.

You are certainly aware of religious practices and traditions that repeat prayers. Chanting and repeating prayers is not used in lieu of Mantras, and they are not a replacement for them, but they are very effective in their own right. I simply wanted to acknowledge chanting because many people know about it.

The last thing about Mantra Meditations. Mantra Meditations are also used by extremely experienced Meditators, so do not think of them as just a beginners' tool. They are a very powerful tool that can be used throughout your Meditative life.

Prayers

Speaking about prayer...Is prayer Meditation? The answer is, it can be, and often is. It tends to be a focused form of Meditation using paradigms (both preferences and constraints) that are particular to the person's religious traditions. One of the advantages to Meditating vs. praying, is that information that does not fit into a particular religious paradigm may come to you in Meditation when it may not in prayer.

Breath Work. Another very effective tool is to use your breath. Using your breath consciously will calm your body and your mind. A "two-fer" so to speak. There are many different Techniques using your breath, and you can take Breath Work workshops for beginners to quite advanced Meditators. We will look at a beginner's use of the Breath.

In its most basic form, simply being aware of your breath, by gently focusing on it, is breath work. Conscious breathing relaxes the body and the mind by relaxing the nervous system. When you focus on your breath, you are not focusing on your 60,000 thoughts.

To use basic breath work in your Meditation, gently focus on your breath in and your breath out. It's very effective *and* portable.

Breath work is specifically used in the Quick Reset Meditation which is used to release immediate Stress quickly. This can be found in Appendix B.

You can study breath work in and out of Meditation. It has produced significant results for many, many people. Andrew Weil, MD's work is one of my favorites for Breath Work study.

Mudras

A Mudra is a way to hold your hands and/or fingers to improve your Meditation experience. Mudras can also involve the body. The science behind them is that an improvement in your mind and bodies' (intentionally plural) energetic connection occurs when you are performing them. There are different mudras for different results. The most common you may be aware of is the mudra held by the Buddha in statues of him. (I say "bodies" because your energetic bodies - Etheric, Astral, and Mental - are intertwined with your physical body as well as your mind and emotions; energetic bodies are a Deep-Dive/Advanced topic which won't be expanded on here, but I wanted you to know of their presence if you were not already aware of them).

What is my experience with Mudras? Probably not quite successful, most likely because I haven't developed the patience to be persistent enough to do them. It is also possible that in this part of my development I have not become sensitive enough to notice their effect. Many of my teachers, but not all, actively use Mudra when they Meditate.

My recommendation. Give them a try but do not let them keep you from Meditating. Many of my Teachers use mudras and many do not. You may find they improve your Meditation experience and you may not notice a difference. Either one is fine.

Here's the real key to successful Meditation: The more people there are Meditating, the easier it gets for any one person to Meditate. (A Deep-Dive topic).

> Key Note: Here's the real key to successful Meditation: The more people there are Meditating, the easier it gets for any one person to Meditate. (A Deep-Dive topic).

Technology-Assisted Meditation

You can use audio or visual devices (CDs, Electronic Eye Coverings) to help put you into a deep Meditative state within minutes. Once learned, you will be able to return to those deep Meditative states within about 20 seconds, without external help. The Monroe Institute, where I first trained, used audio technology to induce deep Meditative states within 20 or 30 seconds. This sounds too good to believe but I spent 6 week-long immersion classes there over 6 or 7 years doing just that. (Information on how to contact the Monroe Institute can be found in Chapter 10).

Guided Meditation. A Guided Meditation is nothing more than someone walking you through a Meditation. If you have anyone read you any of my Meditations in the Appendix while you are in Meditation, you will be doing a Guided Meditation. It's simply someone or something else (CD, podcast, etc.) that walks you through a Meditation. Not all that different than talking to a small child as he or she starts to go to sleep.

Most Guided Meditations are Active Meditations because there is a specific goal to get something for you – finding information or creating an outcome in the Meditation - not just getting you into a Meditative state. But you can use a CD or a friend to guide you into a Passive Meditation without having a further goal. The CD or friend would simply stop speaking after you get into the Meditative state and may resume speaking to bring you back, or pull you out of it, at the end.

Guided Imagery Meditation. Guided Imagery in Meditation is Meditation that is Guided but also uses Visualization. Like Guided Meditation, it is a Technique, not a goal. It is your Meditation Road Map. And in many ways, it can also be your Rosetta Stone.

Guided Imagery Meditation = Guided Meditation + Visualization. The visualization increases the effectiveness of Guided Meditation by about 10,000%. I cannot tell you why that is but I suspect that adding visualization somehow creates a direct link to the subconscious mind and all the power found there.

> Key Note: Guided Imagery Meditation = Guided Meditation + Visualization. The visualization increases the effectiveness of Guided Meditation by about 10,000%.

Most people who start Meditating really, really like it and many stick with it for years. For some, they wish to do more than to just "be" in a really wonderful "space." They have either specific or immediate questions they need answers to, or they want to explore more. Guided Imagery is a very effective Technique to get answers to specific concerns.

I used Guided Imagery in the corporate world to solve business problems. I received very specific guidance in solving these problems. This is why Guided Imagery is one of my very favorite techniques. I will use it in this book to teach you how to pinpoint the causes of Stress in your life, and then use the laser focus to eliminate those causes.

> Key Note: We will use the laser focus of Guided Imagery Meditation to pinpoint your causes of Stress and to eliminate those buggers.

It is possible that once you get into a Meditative state all of the information and understanding you've ever desired will just show up, tap you on the shoulder, and say, "Hi, here we are. Here are all your needs answered. Thanks for coming. Have a great day. Bye." Could it happen? Sure. Is it likely to happen? Not that I've ever heard. Be practical when in Meditation.

What is Guided Imagery? It is like a YouTube video segment without the entertainment. You create in your mind, either by yourself or by using a Guided Meditation, a structure to access information in your Expanded State of Awareness (ESA). Why do you create this structure? Because in an ESA, you will be working from a blank canvas with the most amazing paint palette and an unlimited number of colors and textures. Overlaying a structure onto it and then working within that structure to get answers and results that can only be had in an ESA, gives you the ability to do so. This is extremely important because information that comes in an ESA may not conform to your understanding of reality or how the universe is connected. (Chew on this for a bit).

Key Note: In an ESA, you will be working from a blank canvas with the most amazing paint palette and an unlimited number of colors and textures.

Imagine you are doing your very first Meditation: you've successfully achieved an Expanded State of Awareness, and it looks like....what?........*Nothing you've ever seen before.* In fact, it is so different, you don't recognize what's there until you develop significant skill at doing so. The Expanded State looks just like a blank page. This is what your mind does with information it has not yet learned to process.

**

Did you study about the Pilgrims landing in the New World? The Pilgrims' ships anchored at sea off the coastline, as they could not approach the shore. Had they approached the shore, their ships would have beached, capsized, and never sailed out again. The ships anchored off shore, and the Pilgrims came ashore in large row boats.

American Indians, having built canoes for centuries, recognized the row boats as large canoes. But they had never, ever seen a canoe as large as a sailing ship. So their minds blanked out the ships. In the earliest accounts, the Indians recorded boats coming ashore out of the clouds. That's right, their minds could not process sailing ships so that information was overwritten with clouds, which were large things often seen off shore.

The same thing happens in the Expanded State of Awareness. The mini-video is a trick that allows us to overlay, but not overwrite, a visual story onto the blank canvas of the Expanded State of Awareness, so you can work within it. This is called Guided Imagery.

Example of Using Guided Imagery:

The best way to explain this is to do an example. The first time I Meditated with the intent to meet my Male Inner Essence, I created a mini-video in my mind where I was walking along a fictional path in the woods (which I love to do). I came to a clearing, and off in the distance was a cottage where my Male Inner Essence lived (all of which I made up).

I walked up the steps and knocked on the door. My Male Essence opened it. I asked him what name he wished to be called and we went from there. (Getting his or her name is *much* more important than you would think. I can't exactly say I know why but my intuitive feel is simply common courtesy. If someone you just met turns to you and says, "Hey you, do me this favor," if you are like me, you will not be as receptive to helping as if they said, "Hey [your name], do me this favor," which is completely rude.

Pretty easy, eh? Yes and no. Details and sensations add to the effectiveness of Guided Imagery Meditation (GIM). So once in a Meditative state, using our house and path scenario, take it step by step, as follows:

1. Visualize yourself on such a path. Is the path stone, brick, wood chips, Earth, something else? Is it cool to the feet, hot, sticky, smooth, rough?

2. Consider the types of trees and undergrowth. Can you smell them, can you touch them, can you feel the humidity and temperature? How close are these plants to you?

3. Do this for each segment of your video and be as specific as you can for each of your five senses. Remember, there is no rush. He or she is not going anywhere.

What's your YouTube Video for Meditation? Is it a beach, a desert, a mountain, a field, an ocean, or a town or city? It doesn't matter as long as you set the right intention and walk through the movie.

Here's a good trick: Think of going through Guided Imagery as your first audition for the movie of the year. You've been handed a script, and you need to immerse yourself into the role (which just happens to be you) but the setting is an imaginary scene that you have to bring to life. The Director will *really* be studying how well you bring the surroundings into your character. (By the way, Actors know this work as Role Preparation, and the people who are best at it tend to be the best Actors).

The more in touch you are with the sensations and surroundings of your mini-movie, the deeper you will go into your Meditative State (i.e., Expanded State of Awareness).

To recapture what you will learn and practice here, we will take both of these approaches in this book to reduce Stress:

1. Passively Meditate; and
2. Actively Meditate using the Stress Domino from Chapter 8 and Guided Imagery from Chapter 9.

Passively Meditate -------> to Release Stress
OR
Actively Meditate --------> to Release Stress (more quickly)

SUMMARIZING APPROACHES, TYPES, AND WAYS TO MEDITATE

Remember there are two Approaches to Meditation:

1. Passive and
2. Active

There are many Types (or Goals) of Meditation, for example:

1. Stress Release
2. Body Awareness (Relaxation)
3. Gratitude
4. Forgiveness
5. Self-Love
6. Meeting Inner Essences
7. And 28,000 more....

There are several Techniques (or Ways) used to Meditate, for example:

1. Mantra Meditation
2. Breath Meditation
3. Guided Meditation
4. Guided Imagery Meditation
5. And others......

Three Things to Know:

1. All people and all things, particularly you, are connected to each other in a continuous stream of love;

2. There is more than enough for everybody, including you, regardless of how much or what specific things (including jobs) that other people have; and

3. You can never be harmed and you can never die. At some point your body may wear out or stop working due to disease or injury, yet your energetic you (soul) will always exist.

CHAPTER TWO

BENEFITS TO MEDITATING

*"If you have not yet Meditated,
you are a miracle not yet expressed."
~ C. Chase Carey, MBA*

The benefits to Meditation are numerous. There are many great studies by non-traditional as well as by traditional organizations and schools that statistically document the effects of Meditation. Numerous organizations for the Medical Sciences from Harvard University to the  National Institutes of Health, are devoting significant resources to help quantify the benefits of Meditating. Perhaps your medical or osteopathic doctor does, too.

Living and working in metro Atlanta, Georgia, I am especially fortunate to have Emory University close by. In addition to being an excellent university and medical school, they have partnered with the Dalai Lama to exchange training on Meditation and compassion (from the Dalai Lama's side), and Medical Science/Science (from the Emory side). And they've been doing it since 1998!

Although we don't know <u>all</u> of the benefits of Meditating, it is well documented that Meditating is <u>good</u> for you. We

don't know all of the benefits of physical exercise either, but that doesn't keep us from doing it, does it?

Why Meditate? Because it makes sense. You exercise your body to improve your physical health, and you Meditate to improve your mental clarity and emotional balance.

In addition to having much greater access to information and answers, let's look at some of the specific benefits many people report:

- Stress will be a thing of the *past*. You'll have to turn on the History Channel to learn about it
- Your thoughts will be *sharper*
- Your *creativity* will expand exponentially
- Your emotional responses will be more *balanced*
- Your energy level will *increase*
- You will go through life challenges with much more *ease*
- You will find life to be much more of a *dance* than a series of occurrences
- You will become more *intuitive*
- You will become *less attached* to the smaller details of your life
- You will *sleep better*
- People will respond to you more *positively*
- You will *no longer be affected* by the opinion of others
- You will physically *feel better*

A few of my favorite benefits:

- You'll discover higher realms of existence
- Creativity will rush into the empty space you create by quieting your mind

- You will move from *doing* to *being.* Remember the difference. With *being* there is no performance anxiety; while with *doing* there is <u>always</u> performance anxiety
- Your actions in life will show more congruency with whom you really are and who you desire to be
- Meditation is your "App for Life." There is not one single aspect of you or your life that does not benefit from a good Meditation practice
- Problem solving will be something that comes naturally, not something you have to figure out as you move your life from one problem to the next

And, my all-time favorite (drum roll please): *Synchronicities* will increase in your life at an exponential rate! No sooner will you say to yourself, "Gee, I really need help with such and such," and the next person you bump into will be an expert in that area willing to give you all kinds of help, just because you are you. Your life will become a rich soup of connection.

> Key Note: A great benefit of Meditation is you will move from *doing* something to *being* something. When you are being something, there is no performance anxiety.

Why do these things happen? Internal integration. When all aspects of you are working well together and feeling loved, understood, and accepted, your life moves more freely and effortlessly. Internal integration means your Inner Essences are all working together toward the same goals (see Chapter 9).

Imagine you are the captain of a large ship. You tell your officers where to take the ship, and they have plotters and navigators to determine the ship's course and a host of other crew who run the mechanical and electrical systems of the ship. What happens if some of the crew feel like they are being ignored? They are going to cause problems!

Maybe the problems they cause are not big enough to get them thrown off the ship, but they are big enough so that the ship does not always stay on course and sometimes breaks down or runs aground.

Have you experienced such episodes in your life? Perhaps you've gone on a long road trip with friends or family and each person had their own idea of how you should drive, where you should drive, where and when everybody should eat and where and when everybody should sleep. The external results are one big mess. And by the time you arrive, everybody is worn out because it was just soooo much harder than it ever should have been. As you learn to Meditate you may find that your old, pre-Meditation external life experiences were just a whole lot harder than they should have been. Meditation increases your internal alignment. That can make so many of life's experiences, routine or extraordinary, much smoother.

Key Note: Meditation increases your internal alignment. That can make so many of life's experiences, routine or extraordinary, much smoother.

When we play nice and all get along, we have days filled with joy. When all of you is aligned, you will experience more joy.

Reducing the Frequency and Severity of Breakdowns In Your Life

Do you want to reduce the frequency and severity of the breakdowns in your life? Want to spend less time "in-port" repairing your life circumstances? Meditate.

> Key Note: If you want to reduce the frequency and severity of breakdowns in your life, Meditate.

But there's more...Meditation will give you greater access to information and specific answers to your direct questions.

We're Missing 95%

Around 2008, the Discovery Channel Scientists came out and said that 95% of what exists cannot be seen. 95%. In Meditation's ESA you move directly through the 5% right into the heart of this 95%. Would you like to have access to that unseen and un-accessed 95%? Maybe even just a tiny bit of it? Imagine what you could discover with such access. Imagine what you could do. Imagine what you could be.

> Key Note: Meditation will give you greater access to information and direct answers to your specific questions. You will be able to access the 95% of what is unseen.

It's Not About What Happens IN Meditation

I want to close this chapter with a very important distinction: You can read about and may hear about Meditators who have extraordinary experiences during Meditation. That's fine and good, but why we Meditate is to make changes in our lives OUTSIDE of Meditation.

Very, very few Meditators have extraordinary visions or experiences during Meditations and do not have them outside of Meditation.

Olympic athletes work hard in the gym but don't have extraordinary experiences there. But they do have them OUTside of the gym. They are extraordinary people because what they do IN the gym improves their lives OUTside of the gym. The exact same thing is true about Meditators.

> Key Note: It's not about what happens in your Meditation that counts. It's what happens in your life outside of Meditation that counts. Joy, gratitude, compassion, love, and play are among the most important experiences a person can ever have.

Be Open to an Extraordinary Life

I don't know who said this first, but consider this: What would your life be like if you took time each day to "think about what you cannot imagine?" Can you think of a better place and time to do this than in Meditation? I can't.

<u>Three Things to Know:</u>

1. All people and all things, particularly you, are connected to each other in a continuous stream of love;

2. There is more than enough for everybody, including you, regardless of how much or what specific things (including jobs) that other people have; and

3. You can never be harmed and you can never die. At some point your body may wear out or stop working due to disease or injury, yet your energetic you (soul) will always exist.

CHAPTER THREE

DEALING WITH DISTRACTING THOUGHTS AND PHYSICAL SENSATIONS

"You do not attract what you want, but who you are; often, who you are is often hidden from the conscious mind."
~ C. Chase Carey, MBA

Distracting Thoughts

To have a successful Meditation, one of the first things you want to master is your ability to eliminate distracting thoughts. These thoughts are referred to as Mind Chatter, Monkey Brain, and a thousand other, non-flattering things. These thoughts tend to be things like:

Am I going to get that project at work done on time?
Gee, I wonder what Pete meant after our last date when he said _____.
Man, I need to be on time to pick up the kids tonight.
My boss is an absolute jerk! I am never going to get her to recognize my value!

No matter how much I exercise I just can't seem to lose weight.
And on and on and on........

Not all the thoughts are "bad" of course; hopefully we have many happy thoughts throughout the day. But even happy thoughts are distracting during Meditation because they take our attention away from the Meditation.

There are several good ways to keep Mind Chatter from disrupting your Meditations. Consider that your Mind Chatter, is meaningless as it relates to your Meditation. Many thoughts are meaningless in and of themselves, of course, but give all thoughts no attention as if they were all meaningless during Meditation. The moment you stop being concerned about the meaning of your Mind Chatter is the very first moment it starts to stop bothering you. (This is actually true inside and outside of Meditation).

Any meaning you assign to a thought that does not help you move forward in life is *hurting* you. It is actually as if these thoughts are a constant flow of quick sand, swallowing up your energy, self-esteem, and joy.

Key Note: Only assign meaning to a thought if that meaning helps you in your life.

We are going to look at several good Mind Chatter-distract-me-no-more techniques: the Distraction Box, Mantras (usually silent), Thoughts on a Leaf, and Don't Get in The Car with Them.

Distraction Box

Monkey Brain, Mind Chatter, the little man or woman inside your head, they are all distracting and can be taken care of in the same way. When I studied at the Monroe Institute, they taught me a clever yet simple way to shut down my mind chatter. There they taught me to mentally visualize a box in my mind into which I was to throw all of my distracting thoughts. They refer to the box as an Energy Conversion Box. I simply think of it as a Distraction Box.

Here's what my Distraction Box looks like to me:

Putting your distractions into such a box is going to take practice. Do not be frustrated by it. Just practice putting every distracting thought into the box and shut the lid tight. Every single time a distracting thought comes into your mind, visualize the thought going into the box and snapping the lid shut!

I have a special trick that I use with my Distraction Box. My Distraction Box has a vacuum attached to the bottom of the box. Why? Because I found those little distracting thoughts kept slipping back out so my solution was to suck them back in. Hah! I won. (True story.)

> Key Note: At some point in your Meditation practice, you will discover that some of the small, distracting thoughts are actually *information* coming to you.

Mantras

We spoke of these earlier and they are worth repeating. Remember that a Mantra is a sound or a series of sounds (silent or not) that help to move your attention from mental distractions to mental quiet and openness. Mantras are believed to assist in spiritual growth as well, which they very likely may do. The best Mantras are simple and have no particular meaning to the Meditator, so he can use it to reduce mind chatter without creating meaning around another thought. Mantras can be very helpful in assisting people to not be affected by distractions, but they are not necessary to get through this area.

Mantras can be an excellent way for beginning Meditators to keep their mind chatter at bay.

Thoughts on a Leaf

Both one of the simplest and most effective means of keeping mind chatter from keeping you from a clear minded Meditation is to visualize your thoughts landing on leaves, the leaves landing on a stream, and then the leaves gently floating away. You can also visualize the thoughts as the leaves themselves. I do not know whose idea this was but thanks to students mentioning it, it is a method I use frequently in workshops.

Don't Get in The Car with Them

Margaret Mills, a fellow Meditation teacher and IBM Resiliency Consultant, teaches her students a very clever way to keep distracting thoughts from distracting them. She says to view distracting thoughts as though they were traffic that is passing through your mind. Don't assign any meaning or additional thought to the traffic. And since it is your brain's job to think, it is only doing its job and passing that information off to your mind, and that's okay. She simply asks students to realize that even if the distracting thoughts are driving through your mind, you have an important choice: you do *not* have to get in the car and go with them!

How simple is this? Margaret is a brilliant teacher and I share her method here with her permission.

> Key Note: You can choose to get caught up in the emotions and events of your life or you can decide to stay in your calm center - your core - your soul - your true consciousness. You get to decide.

Breath Work

Just as we discussed Mantras earlier, Breath Work bears repeating.

When distracted in your Meditation, you can get back to stillness by simply shifting your attention to your breath. Let's try it right now:

- Shift your attention to your breath.

- Shift your attention to your breath.

- Shift your attention to your breath.

Relaxed now? Mind clear? You bet.

Physical Distractions

Physical distractions are just as important to deal with as distracting thoughts, but a whole lot simpler to handle. Let's take a look at how to deal with the most common physical distractions:

What Happens If/When…

1. You have an itch? …..Scratch it
2. You have to urinate?…..Get up and pee
3. You have to sneeze?…..Sneeze
4. You have to move around?….Move around, but not a lot, particularly if you are Meditating with other people
5. If the sensation is still annoying you, try focusing on another part of your body, like your right little toe, for instance. Or simply go back to focusing on your breath.

Are you picking up on where I am going with this?

Should you ever get into a Meditation and the physical (or thought) distractions become too distracting, simply come back to waking consciousness, closing the Meditation gently. Go on about your day or evening. Remember, you'll Meditate again and there is nothing that says you have to complete 100% of the Meditations you start.

> Key Note: Should you ever try to Meditate and the mental or physical distractions become too distracting, simply come back to waking consciousness, closing the Meditation gently. Go on about your day or evening. Try again tomorrow.

<u>Three Things to Know:</u>

1. All people and all things, particularly you, are connected to each other in a continuous stream of love;

2. There is more than enough for everybody, including you, regardless of how much or what specific things (including jobs) that other people have; and

3. You can never be harmed and you can never die. At some point your body may wear out or stop working due to disease or injury, yet your energetic you (soul) will always exist.

CHAPTER FOUR

HOW TO MEDITATE - THE 5 STEPS TO A PERFECT MEDITATION

"You are more than your physical body." ~ Bob Monroe

To Meditate, you need to do (up to) 5 things. And 5 things only. Let's take a quick look at the 5:

Passive Meditation (Steps 1-3, Sometimes 4 - It's a Gray Area)

1. Quiet / Relax your body
2. Quiet / Relax your mind (at this point you will begin to move into an Expanded State of Awareness)
3. Move into an Expanded State of Awareness – through focused intent

Active Meditation (Add Steps 4 - 5)

4. Create an Intention
5. Use a Road Map - Guided Meditation or Guided Imagery Meditation

So far, so good, right? Let's look at these in a bit more detail:

But first, find a Special Place to Meditate - Staging

I used to label good Meditative Staging – setting yourself a good, comfortable, quiet, disturbance free, safe place to Meditate - as the first step in Meditation. That's because it is so very important for beginning students to learn. But I changed recently because once you become proficient at Meditating, your staging will not affect you nearly as much. This is a little tricky to explain because you will want to have good Meditative Staging, but over time you will develop the skill level such that when you Meditate on a train, a bus, a plane, a waiting room, etc., it will be just as effective as if you were Meditating at your special place at home or at your office.

Let's talk about effective staging. Find a quiet, comfortable place where you will *not be disturbed.* You can sit, recline, or lie down. There is no best way to have your body positioned when you Meditate; chose the position that is best for you. Don't be concerned with what other people do. (Occasionally I lay down simply because it can be more comfortable for me, but *most* people who do so tend to fall asleep.)

Once you've Meditated regularly for a while you will be able to Meditate in more places with more distractions without a problem. Actually, for consistent Meditators, their life becomes a living Meditation. But when you start, spend some effort with your staging. Occasionally I work as an Extra in TV (Drop Dead Diva, Necessary Roughness) and Movies (A&E's Coma). You would absolutely *not* believe how much time and effort goes into setting up a scene, meaning furniture positioning, windows, colors, textures, and yes, lightning, *way, way, way* before any actor ever walks onto the set. The entertainment industry employs many extremely talented professionals at a high cost to do staging. Why? Because it makes a *huge* difference to what you, the audience, experiences. You just don't realize it.

So back to your staging. I would like you to work on the ability to Meditate sitting up or gently reclining; it will accelerate your ability to receive information during your Meditation and remain alert.

Don't Go To the Light

This is important: You will also want to be in a dimly lit area and use an eye pillow or other eye covering – as dark and as completely covering the eye as possible (100% compliance with this is tough for me due to my nose, which is, shall I say, large).

Again, this is very important and I don't want you to miss this step as many people do. The Pineal Gland, which is in the center of your head (as opposed to the center of your brain), is the most important physical organ for your intuitive skills. This wonderful little gland works best when there is complete darkness to your eyes. As a test, ask yourself if you are able to dream in a brightly lit room. Doesn't work, does it?

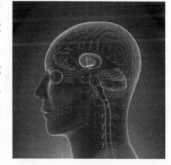

> Key Note: You will want to be in a dimly lit area and use an eye pillow or other eye covering – as dark and as completely covering the eye as possible.

Clothing

Wear something comfortable, not restrictive, that you do not use for other tasks. Just as you might put on comfy pajamas when you go to bed at night, it sets the mood. Wearing the same or similar type of clothing during your Meditation can help send a signal to your body and mind that it is time to quiet, but not sleep, so no PJs.

And let's not forget background music. Almost any of the Metamusic ™ CDs from the Monroe Institute work quite well. Background music is not necessary, but it can help quiet the mind. Just be cautious not to use music with words or popular tunes because you will start to focus on the words and sing away (let my mistakes be to your benefit). If you are in a place where you can experience Nature's sounds, *please*, skip the music. There is no music more beautiful and connecting as nature's sounds. In fact, the Monroe Institute (www.MonroeInstitute.org) uses ocean sounds (their ocean CD is called "Surf") as background sound on a great deal of their training audios.

Pets

If you like pets, you will like Meditation. And your pets will like you while you Meditate. It is really hard to stop your pets from visiting you if they want to and there is no one else in the house to distract them. So let them visit. At first their visits will be distracting but their "interference" will actually provide you excellent practice with maintaining a Meditative space while experiencing external distractions. One of our cats, Montana, used to sleep at my feet when I Meditated. In addition to keeping my feet warm, I considered it a great honor because of something Eckhart Tolle said in *The Power of Now:* "I have lived with several Zen Masters; all of them cats".

1. Quiet / Relax Your Body

Get into a comfortable position (if sitting, hips above knees). If you sit, do so with your legs crossed as it is a more stable position than having your legs out in front of you. You will want a pad or a blanket on the floor to shield you from the cold and you will want a pad, cushion, or pillow to sit on, on top of the blanket, so your hips are above your knees.

Zafus and Zabutons

Pads you can purchase specifically for Meditation are called zafus and zabutons. A zafu is a round Meditation cushion that you put on top of a zabuton, which is a square-ish, thinner cushion. The zafu sits on top  of the zabuton and then you sit on top of both. The zabuton insulates you from the temperature of the floor and the zafu gets your hips above your knees. You can get a combination of these for under $70, if you want to go high end. The pic to the right is of them.

How to your relax your body. There are many ways but I will share my favorite: Squiggle around (very important) and focus on your breathing. Listen and feel your breath as it comes in and out, just the same as the ocean waves come in and out. Don't think about your breath and don't take deeper, shallower, longer or shorter breaths; just breathe. This listening also is a great form of background music.

Focusing on your breathing at any time day or night will bring great relaxation and rejuvenation to your mind, emotions, and body. Breathing and Breath Work is so very important that you could spend hundreds of hours just studying and working with your breath. You can achieve amazing Meditations with advanced Breath Work. I am not spending much time on Breath Work here so we can keep the pace moving, but I do not want you to underestimate the effectiveness of Breath Work.

> Key Note: Advanced skill in Breath Work can add to your Meditative experience. It is one of many ways to do so. There are others which are just as effective.

Second, I visualize receiving a massage, starting with my feet and working my way up to my head. First, my feet get a deep massage, and then the feet relax as the massage works up to my lower legs. A few moments of massage on my lower legs and then upward to my knees; as this happens, my lower legs relax. Repeat the process all the way up to the top of your head.

Becca's Butter Body

A student of mine shared a great idea during class and I share it here with you: View your body as being made of a stick of butter, getting a warm massage. Once the warm massage has worked an area, such as your feet, *visualize* and *feel* that part of your body melting away. Start at your feet and work all the way up to the top of your head until your body has completely melted away. (Thanks Becca!)

You'll love this, I promise.

There is also a great Bruce Lee teaching that I love which can help you in relaxing your body:

> "Empty your mind, be formless, shapeless - like water. Now you put water into a cup, it becomes the cup, you put water into a bottle, it becomes the bottle, you put it in a teapot, it becomes the teapot. Now water can flow or it can crash. Be water, my friend."

Many people think of Bruce Lee as a cheesy, B-movie martial artist. In reality he was one of the most accomplished martial artists of all time. Most all of today's best martial artists study his work endlessly.

2. Quiet / Relax Your Mind

This step is almost always the biggest challenge for those new to Meditating.

Your goal is to first eliminate the disturbance caused by the big, distracting thoughts in your mind and then continue on to eliminate all the smaller distracting thoughts, most often referred to as Mind Chatter or Monkey Brain. This takes practice, practice, and then more practice. Mastering this, which you *will* do, is crucial to successful a Meditation.

Remember the tools we've discussed so far?

- Create a distraction box
- Use a mantra
- Use your breath
- Thoughts on a leaf
- Don't get in the car with them

3. Move into an Expanded State of Awareness

Hard to explain but fairly simple to do. After you have quieted and relaxed your body and mind, have a soft focus. A loose attention. Be open to new experiences and information. Your mind will naturally move into an ESA.

You may wish to look at it like this: There is a saying going around that "We are spiritual beings having a human experience." I do not know the author but I love the phrase. If you look at life this way, consider that if we come from a spiritual realm, what would that look like? Largely energetic and largely a much expanded understanding, would be my guess. So here we are cruising around the universe as energetic aspects and all of a sudden we are pushed and squeezed into this thing called a human being. A bag of watery liquid that is hard and soft at the same time, but for sure it is a lot more restrictive than what we were just experiencing. All of a sudden we are not cruising so freely and our expanded state has become a squeezed bag of organic molecules.

Meditation takes your focus, your soft attention, right out back to our energetic selves: back to the ESA where we originated from: back to less squeeze and fewer molecules. Kind of like what? Like where you belong. This movement into an ESA is a natural movement "back" to who you really are.

4. Create an Intention.

Whenever you do anything in your life, you start out with an intention. When you get up in the morning your intention may be to get ready for work, get the kids ready for school, get ready to exercise, open your business, or simply to have a relaxing day. Why do you do this?

Because Intention creates Attention. Attention creates Action. Action creates Results.

> Key Note: Intention ------> Attention. Attention ------> Action. Action ------> Results

If you do not start an activity with an intention, it will be sheer luck if that activity happens well or even happens at all. A ship's captain always leaves port with an intention, right?

The same is true when you Meditate. Maybe during a Meditation your intention is to simply relax, maybe it is to bring your mind, emotions, and body into more harmony, or maybe it is to get specific answers to specific questions.

Another thing: Remember that Meditation can be purposeful (focused) inquiry during an Expanded State of Awareness, not just "being" in an Expanded State of Awareness. In this Expanded

State lie great resources as well as influences. Some influences may provide less than helpful assistance to your Meditation so we want to ask for protection from such influences.

Let's take a look at what an Intention could be: (say this in your mind or out loud)

"I intend to experience/understand/get introduced to ___ during this Meditation. I ask for protection from non-beneficial influences."

If you want to be clever, expand your Intention to deal with distractions, like this:

"I intend to experience/understand/get introduced to _____ during this Meditation. I ask for protection from non-beneficial influences. Any distractions during this Meditation will enhance my experience, not deflect from it."

5. Go After Something Using Your Road Map (Guided or Guided Imagery Meditation)

We are going to use Guided Imagery so you can navigate your questions to the very best place in your Expanded State of Awareness. Guided Imagery, which is given more detail in Chapter 9, provides such a road map.

Can you Meditate without it? Absolutely. You can Passively Meditate (Steps 1-3). You can just be "open" and quiet during a Meditation rather than seek specific answers. And it's great to do that, really great. In fact, Passive Meditation is the most common form of Meditation in the world which is a really big place.

For people in businesses or organizations looking to solve problems, Active Meditation is much more effective.

When I first started Meditating I had significant health issues, so I used Active Meditation because I was after very specific answers to very specific problems. My problems were quite challenging and very disruptive to a productive life. Therefore, about 85% or more of my Meditations used Guided Imagery and 15% or so didn't. Plus, being new to Meditation, I had a lot to learn about the structure of the "Expanded State of Awareness."

Today I use Active Meditation a bit less for two reasons: 1) Sometimes I just want to let go and enjoy the Meditative State without trying to solve a specific problem, which makes the experience not unlike a spa day for my mind and emotion; and, 2) I am more skilled at accepting structures and concepts presented to me during Expanded Awareness so I receive significant direction during Passive Meditation. You will too as you become more experienced with Meditation.

Particularly for newer people, Guided Imagery gives you a significant leg up on getting where you want to go and getting you what you want once you get there, if you have very specific targets in mind. That's proven thousands of times a day throughout the world, perhaps tens of thousands of times, each and every day, but it is not for everyone every day.

> Key Note: Particularly for newer people, Guided Imagery gives you a significant leg up on getting where you want to go and getting what you want once you get there, if you have very specific targeted questions.

Dalai Lama and NY Hot Dog Vender:

Okay, now for some comic relief. This is a joke about the Dalai Lama and the NY Hot Dog Vendor....

On the way to give a speech to the UN, the Dalai Lama got hungry and asked his driver to pull over to the curb to a street vendor. He jumped out, and said to the hot dog vendor, "Make me one with everything." The hot dog vendor pulled out a plump dog, slapped it into a bun, smothered it with ketchup, mustard, relish, and handed it to the Dalai Lama.

The hot dog vendor said, "That'll be $5 dollars, Your Holiness."

The Dalai Lama handed him a $20 bill, which the vendor promptly stuffed in his pocket, and then turned to help another hungry customer.

The Dali Lama, taken aback, said, "Hey, hot dog vendor, how about my change?"

The hot dog vendor stopped, turned slowly toward the Dalai Lama and said, "Your Holiness, change comes from within."

(Author is unknown but very much appreciated).

A Longer Term Skill is Mind Awake, Body Asleep

For consistent Meditators, particularly those who are used to Guided or Guided Imagery Meditation, you may find that you may reach the skill level where you are **completely awake, your mind clear, and your body completely quieted, even asleep.**

It would be okay that your body is asleep so long as your mind is still clear and alert. Think you cannot do this? Sure you can. You do it every time you dream.

Funny story. One birthday my wife booked a couples massage for the both of us. About 20 minutes in, my body was dead asleep. So asleep, in fact, that it started to snore. And when I snore, the dead know it. A great gift I inherited from my father, which drove my mother crazy.

Okay, back to the massage: I'd been Meditating about 15 years by that point, much of it Guided with a live person managing me. So, you guessed it. While my body was asleep during the massage my mind was clear and alert. I heard myself snoring and then I heard my wife apologize to her massage therapist about my snoring. So I calmly said to my wife, "Just because my body is asleep doesn't mean I can't hear you." My wife and the two massage therapists were so stunned, you could have heard a pin drop 20 miles away.

People don't realize that the mind and the body can and do act independently.

This concept is a brain twister for many people, and it takes a lot of practice. I will not kid you about that. But it's great and you will love it, should you develop that skill. For now, just let the concept settle in.

Key Note: People don't realize that the mind and the body can and do act independently. Think "Mind Awake, Body Asleep."

 and

How Often Should You Meditate?

Almost all teachers will tell you to Meditate each and every day. I won't tell you that.

But I will tell you that if you Meditate each and every day, you will love it and you will *not* want to go a day without it. For most people who wish to Meditate, if they are "forced" to jump in on day one Meditating each and every day, they experience resistance and Meditation for them, at first, will often feel like a burden.

It's the new millennium. Many people do not have cookie cutter days. And many people have activities that start with work in the morning and end with family or friend activities late at night. Add to that that you really cannot Meditate within 2 hours of consuming alcohol, it gets tricky to Meditate each and every day.

Here's my recommendation: When you first start to Meditate shoot for 3 – 4 times a week for 3 weeks. And from there consider Meditating each day. At some point, within the first month or two of your Meditation practice, definitely get in 3 weeks of daily Meditation. Your skills, enjoyment, and benefits of Meditating will be greatly increased. By the way, never beat up on yourself for missing a day of Mediation. (Don't ever beat yourself up for anything, for that matter.)

A easy, but not inappropriate, short cut is to use Technology Assisted Meditation as with the Monroe Institute Hemi-Sync™ CDs. These CDs use audio technology that will put you into a deep Meditative state within 20 seconds and the CD will keep you there until the end at which time it brings you back out of the ESA to waking consciousness. Sometimes, particularly after a busy or challenging day, I just don't *feel* like getting myself into a Meditative state and being there. My solution? I pop on headphones, pull up a Monroe CD on my playlist, and bam! I am G-O-N-E. And there are a lot of 22 minute Meditations so it's not only easy and effective, it's quick. I ALWAYS FEEL GREAT after using a Monroe CD. This is how I learned to Meditate in the early 1990s.

Make no mistake, Meditating every day will greatly enhance your life. This is very, very important so I will restate it:

Meditating every day will greatly enhance your life.

How Long Should You Meditate During Meditation?

There is a lot of study that Meditating twice a day for 20 minutes will be extremely beneficial. I know many people that do this and I know many that Meditate just once a day for 30 or 40 minutes and I know many people that Meditate once a day for about 60 minutes.

What works for you is what works for you. Personally, I tend to Meditate about 40-45 minutes once a day. Sometimes though, I "only" Meditate for 20 minutes and sometimes I Meditate for 90 minutes.

When I was in intense study I Meditated every day for 1 hour and twice a day on weekends for 90 minutes each time, no lie. That period lasted at least 2 years. Did I benefit by that? You bet I did. But understand that for me, Meditation was and is something I am deeply passionate about and interested in. So for me, it was not only something I wanted to use to benefit me, but it was something I wanted to understand deeply so I could share it with others.

Three Things to Know:

1. All people and all things, particularly you, are connected to each other in a continuous stream of love;

2. There is more than enough for everybody, including you, regardless of how much or what specific things (including jobs) that other people have; and

3. You can never be harmed and you can never die. At some point your body may wear out or stop working due to disease or injury, yet your energetic you (soul) will always exist.

CHAPTER FIVE

DURING MEDITATION, GOOD HABITS AND GOOD QUESTIONS TO ASK

"You should sit in meditation for 20 minutes a day, unless you're too busy; then you should sit for an hour."
~ Old Zen saying

Meditation is a practice that has few param-eters. It really can't be done wrong and a person can gain insight on virtually anything they choose. In fact, I joke with my students that to date, OSHA has reported absolutely NO accidents at work due to Meditation. It just cannot get safer than that!

Key Note: To date, OSHA has reported absolutely NO accidents at work due to Meditation. It just cannot get safer than that!

To get good results, as with anything else you do, there are things that help and things that do not help. Given this, there are a several good do's and don'ts for beginning and seasoned

Meditators. The reason for this is that you will soon learn that the quiet space you create with an Expanded State of Awareness is a pretty cool place to hang out.

During Meditation, if you ask for insight in some aspect of your life, you will very likely get a response; sometimes it comes right away, sometimes it comes later on, or it comes bit by bit. Meditation is a long-term *relationship* you build with yourself, so you don't need to answer every challenge in your life in the first week.

> Key Note: The quiet space you create with an Expanded State of Awareness is a pretty cool place to hang out. Meditation is a long term *relationship* you build with yourself.

So let's look at some good things:

Good Habits and Good Questions to Ask

Good Habits start with Good Staging. You must have a comfortable, dimly lit, quiet, respected place to Meditate.

Here are the things that can help you, particularly when you begin:

1. Meditate in the same place and at the same time of day if you can, until you are quite comfortable with Meditating.

2. If there are other people living with you, let them know you are NOT to be disturbed and they are to be quiet while you are Meditating, period, no exceptions (issues of health aside).

3. Keep special items in your Meditation area/room. I like handmade objects, objects made from wood or stone, and of course, just about any craft item my daughter made for me growing up in school. Pictures are nice too.

4. Write things down afterwards. Much information comes in the form of symbols, physical objects, and feelings. Their meaning may only make sense at a future date.

5. Keep the space/area respected. Others are not to tramp through it, leave things there, or disturb what is there for you. The absolutely most important thing to each and every human being should be their connection with themselves and Nature. Your special space provides the foundation for that.

Key Note: The absolutely most important thing to each and every human being should be their connection with themselves and Nature.

Good Habits Require Good Questions. Be smart and balanced - and OPEN - to the information you receive.

There are so many things you can ask in Meditation, but what you get back and how reliable that information is, is often *directly* related to your intent and skill in asking the question. If your approach to a question is a desire through desperation, you stand a good chance of getting a poor quality of information back. (The details to this subject are appropriately handled in more advanced study).

Here are Good Questions to Ask:

1. What is the most important thing for me to know?
2. Are there any physical issues that need my attention?
3. I want to do such and such. What is your view of that for me?
4. What should I be aware of that I am not expecting?
5. What could be my next step in life? What should I consider around this?
6. I have such and such problem/challenge at work, school, home that I have been unable to work through. Please tell me what I am missing.
7. What are the key needs of my Inner Essences? (Advanced; Chapter 9)
8. Which Inner Essence needs to be addressed first? (Advanced; Chapter 9)
9. What is the biggest misunderstanding I have?
10. What is the most important thing for me to know about my children, spouse, parents, friends, co-workers?

Three Things to Know:

1. All people and all things, particularly you, are connected to each other in a continuous stream of love;

2. There is more than enough for everybody, including you, regardless of how much or what specific things (including jobs) that other people have; and

3. You can never be harmed and you can never die. At some point your body may wear out or stop working due to disease or injury, yet your energetic you (soul) will always exist.

CHAPTER SIX

DURING MEDITATION, BAD HABITS AND BAD QUESTIONS TO ASK

"It's never too late to be who you might have been."
~ George Eliot

The camel has two humps, so let's look at the flip side of good things to do and ask. Like the fellow above who just doesn't seem to get that not everything you <u>can</u> do, you <u>should</u> do, let's sprinkle a bit of caution to your Meditation practice...

Bad Habits and Bad Questions to Ask

Do you want to have an <u>uns</u>uccessful Meditative session? Start with Bad Habits.

Bad Habits start with Bad Staging. Remember, you must have a comfortable, dimly lit, quiet, respected place to Meditate.

Here are the things that can destroy your ability to Meditate successfully:

1. Meditating in bed
2. Meditating in front of the TV
3. Meditating in a noisy area
4. Meditating where you will be interrupted
5. Meditating in different places and at different times (As you advance your skills, learning to Meditate anywhere, anytime is actually a key skill)

> Key Note: Learning to Meditate anywhere, anytime, is a key success milestone.

Bad Habits continue with Bad Questions. Don't start from desperation, frustration, anger, or revenge, even though you may have those challenges. RELAX, first and foremost. Few significant changes happen overnight, although I encourage you to believe in Miracles.

Here are Bad Questions to Ask:

1. When will I become rich, get married, get pregnant, be healthy? Instead, ask: I desire to be wealthy, married, pregnant, healthy. What do you advise for me to do to accomplish this/that?

2. When will I die? (Any answer you think you get will be incorrect).

3. I really do not like X person/company/organization/government and really want to make their life messy for what they

did to me. What's the best way to do that? (This makes great TV but lousy Meditation).

4. How should I invest my money?*

5. What are tonight's winning lottery numbers?*

*A special note on numbers 4 and 5. You can ask these questions, but my experience and the experience of many teachers is that, for whatever reason, the answers given rarely work. What you want to avoid when asking for financial advice is to assume the advice is absolutely correct, inside *information for you*. You'd end up flying off to Las Vegas, putting all your money on one number and losing it all. You'd end up just like the guy on the GEICO commercial who had to sell his hair!

Don't be the guy selling his hair.

Three Things to Know:

1. All people and all things, particularly you, are connected to each other in a continuous stream of love;

2. There is more than enough for everybody, including you, regardless of how much or what specific things (including jobs) that other people have; and

3. You can never be harmed and you can never die. At some point your body may wear out or stop working due to disease or injury, yet your energetic you (soul) will always exist.

PART TWO - REMOVING STRESS (AKA STRESS NO MORE!)

CHAPTER SEVEN

ANATOMY OF STRESS AND THE UNDERLYING FEAR BANK

"The illiterate of the 21st century will not be those who cannot read and write, but those who cannot learn, unlearn, and relearn."
~ Alvin Toffler

What is Stress?

When you want to deal with something, you do so by first understanding how it works and then working that process to improve the situation to your liking. Let me share with you three things few people recognize about the conditions required to be Stressed:

The 3 Conditions Required for Stress to Exist

1. Stress is some part of you feeling **Threatened**.

2. When you are under Stress, you are living in the presence of an **Active Fear**.

3. When you are under Stress, there is a perception (real or not real) of **Uncertainty**.

> Key Note: Stress is some part of you feeling Threatened. Stress is living in the presence of an Active Fear. Stress occurs when there is the perception (real or not real) of Uncertainty.

Most people are aware of many of their fears but not aware of them all because not all are Active or Actively Expressed at any one time (*phew!*), and some may never be expressed if we don't have an external stimulus to activate that particular Stress.

Let's Look at Some Examples

Example. Lacy is afraid of flying. She never thinks of flying because she never travels far. She always takes a car or train to where she needs to go in the few instances she travels more than a few miles from home.

Question: Does Lacy have a fear of flying? The answer is YES.

Question: Is Lacy stressed about flying? The answer is NO. She never flies.

Question: Lacy just found out she has a job interview 2,000 miles away tomorrow and the only way to get there is to fly.

Is Lacy now Stressed? YES! Why? Because her fear of flying became Active.

Question: What caused her to be Stressed? An external activator, accepting the job interview, triggered her Fear of Flying to become activated.

Lacy could be afraid of a million other things: heights, fish, turtles - who knows? But if she lives in the flat desert with no mountains, no fish, and no turtles, she is not aware that she is afraid of these things and will not be Stressed by them because there is no external activator.

Why Get Rid of Stress in the First Place?

Why get rid of stress in the first place? **Because a lot of Stress is created around avoiding shame, embarrassment, and loss of identity or affinity, or not getting the approval we want.** Do not model your life around these Fears – they can wreak havoc with you and can lead to death. Fear of being shamed, embarrassed, or losing your identity or not getting approval is predominant in Western societies and is the number one motivator of most actions or inactions people take. The result is that people are not themselves, and there is nothing less attractive than you being the person you are not. **Fear is a four letter word and should be treated as such: not tolerated in your life.**

> Key Note: A lot of Stress is created around avoiding shame, embarrassment, and loss of identity or affinity, or not getting the approval we want. Do not model your life around these Fears – they can wreak havoc with you and can lead to death.

Key Note: Fear is a four letter word and should be treated as such: not tolerated in your life.

The Fastest and Healthiest Way to Release Stress Immediately

Go to sleep and to stay asleep. This will give your body, mind (in your brain) and emotions (in your heart) the time and protected space to come to peace with the stressful situation.

When you awake, some of the stress will be gone and you will be much more able to do what you have to do in a calm, clear way.

How long you need to sleep depends on the situation specifics and time of day. For many people and situations, 1 ½-2 hours will do it; for tougher difficulties or those occurring at night, a good night's sleep is important. Unless you are a first responder, most people have no immediate action they can take to eliminate the Stress, particularly if it involves the loss of a job, a home, a dear friend, a loved animal, or a desired opportunity. Sleep is viewed subconsciously by your body as a safe place, a healing place. Do you remember getting comfy on a cold night, jumping into your PJs and then snuggling under the covers? Your body does, and it loved every one of those nights.

> Key Note: The Fastest and Healthiest Way to Release Stress Immediately is to go to sleep and to stay asleep.

Remember, however, that not all Stress is bad. Sarah McLean, one of my Meditation Teachers, used to work for the Army in a health capacity, and part of that work included understanding Stress on the battlefield. She learned that some level of *controlled* Stress is critical to success in difficult situations. Fortunately, very few of us will ever be on an active battlefield, but if controlled Stress makes soldiers safer, imagine what it can do for people like you and me.

> Key Note: Some level of *controlled* Stress is critical to success in difficult situations. If controlled Stress makes soldiers safer on the battlefield, imagine what it can do for people like you and me.

If you were... correction, <u>when</u> you are free of your Fears, you will be not affected by the opinion of others. Again, when you are free of your Fears, you will be not affected by the opinion of others. Imagine how wonderful that will be!

> Key Note: Fear of being shamed, embarrassed, or losing your identity is predominant in Western societies and is the number one motivator of most actions or inactions people take. The result is that people are not them-selves, and there is nothing is more beautiful than the person you are, and there is nothing less attractive than you being the person you are not.

What is Fear?

Fear is a reaction from your subconscious mind, and sometimes conscious mind, that you are going to do something it really doesn't want you to do, or that something is going to happen to you that it really doesn't want to happen.

The Fear reaction is your response-conclusion after running the perceived threat through your belief systems. Your belief systems are the sum total of the interpretations and conclusions drawn by you from experience, education, and the influence of others.

Key Note: Fear is a reaction, often from your subconscious mind, that you are going to do something it really doesn't want you to do, or that something is going to happen to you that it really doesn't want to happen to you.

Here's what it looks like:

External Event --->

Processed Through Your Belief Systems ---->

Your Reaction/Non-Reaction

Fears add up over time and we (unconsciously) "save" them like they are money. We put them in our Fear Bank which we start

building up from a very young age, comprised monthly of other things that were taught to us and a few misinterpretations we made along the way. But Fears aren't money. They are more like energy-draining, debt-collecting leaches. Now, do you want to build up a big balance in your Fear Bank, or do you want to burn the little suckers off you like the energy-leaches that they are?

Burn them off! Good answer!

> Key Note: Fears add up over time and we (unconsciously) "save" them like they are money. We put them in our Fear Bank which we start building up from a very young age. They are energy-draining leaches. Let's burn them off!

A Fear can be a reaction to a real threat, or it may be a reaction to a perceived threat that may or may not be true. All threats are perceived on a subconscious or conscious level, but depending on the specific threat, your past experiences, your belief system, and a dozen other things, the Fear may be more connected with your subconscious mind or more with your conscious mind.

Examples of Stress and Their Fears

Example. Ken decides to take his family to Hawaii for vacation. His wife is deathly afraid of snakes and is nervous about the trip. But she goes along because, after all, Hawaii is Hawaii.

She is anxious about the trip during the weeks of planning and during the flight. The closer the plane gets to Hawaii, the more stressed she becomes (because she is getting closer to the snakes). During the flight she is handed a customs form from the Hawaiian Agricultural Department. One of the questions on the form is about bringing in live animals. An odd question, his wife thinks, until the flight attendant explains that there are no snakes in Hawaii.

Ken's wife is immediately relieved and her Fear of snakes goes away.

Question: Is the threat real? NO.

Question: Did Ken's wife act as if it were real even though there was absolutely no evidence on earth that there was such a threat to her? YES.

Question: Why? Because her belief systems understood there to be snakes in Hawaii.

Question: Once Ken's wife realized there were no snakes in Hawaii, did her Fear of snakes go away? NO. It became In-Active, but did not leave. It only *appeared* to have gone away.

Question: Once Ken's wife realized there were no snakes in Hawaii, why did she stop being stressed? Because the Fear was no longer an Active Fear.

Key Note: Stress is living in the presence of an Active Fear.

Question: Does it matter if the threat is real or simply perceived? NO. As long as a part of your mind believes the threat is real, you will react to the external event as if it were real.

Example. Rebecca decides to create a painting with old toxic paints instead of using newer, non-toxic latex paints. She may do this because she ran out of the newer paint. The toxic paint triggers a subconscious fear of poisoning. Rebecca becomes Stressed or anxious.

Question: Is the threat real?

Answer: YES. But it may or may not be very likely with limited exposure. If Rebecca accidentally ate some of her mom's old paint when she was a child and ended up in the Emergency Room getting her stomach pumped, it may make great sense to her both consciously and subconsciously, and therefore she exhibits more Stress.

Remember, Stress is living in the presence of an Active Fear.

Question: Does it matter if the threat is real or simply perceived?

Answer: NO. As long as a part of your mind believes the threat is real, you will react to the external event as if it were real.

Someone once said: Fears are False Expectations Appearing Real. This is often exactly what goes on. A Fear can be derived one of two ways:

1. Real Fear - based on fact.

2. False Fear - based on incorrect fact or misinterpretation of information.

Before we move on, let's recap what we've learned about how Stress comes to be:

- First. There is an external event. E.g., Potential travel, potential snake;
- Second. You consciously or subconsciously process the information though your belief systems (some of which are unconscious);
- Third: You come to a conclusion about the external event and either react to the conclusion or not.

The Three Universal Illusions (Lies) Whose Belief Creates Every Form of Stress

This is where it gets fun.

Everything you or anyone else Fears is a reaction (subconscious or conscious) to one of the three Universal Beliefs:

1. You are absolutely alone and not connected to anybody or anything; you are separated from love;

2. There is a very limited amount of everything that exists. If you do not get it and get it now, there won't be enough left for you; and

3. You can be harmed or killed and then you will be no more or even more alone than you are now.

These Lies we have been telling ourselves have been around for a long time. They are supported by an energetic template which reinforces the sharing of them and makes it easier for new people to buy into them (a Deep Dive / Advanced Topic).

All Fears that you and I experience are derivatives (children) of these Universal (parent) Lies. Let's look at some of our common Fears and identify the parent Universal Lie(s) they are tied to:

- Fear of flying....#3
- Fear of not enough money....#2
- Fear of being alone....#1
- Fear of public speaking....#1
- Fear of spiders....#3
- Fear of being naked in public....#1
- Fear of being shamed....#1

Pretty straightforward, isn't it? Kind of amazing that it doesn't take years of study to understand the basic structure of Fears. Understanding the three Lies we all believe in, that cause all Fears, will help you to release the fear more easily. You will still target the specific Fear rather than the apparent Lie to release the Fear. However, working with the apparent Lies in Meditation, an Advanced Topic, can be quite enlightening.

> Key Note. The Fear reaction is your response-conclusion after running the perceived threat through your belief systems. Your belief systems are the sum total of the interpretations and conclusions drawn by you from experience, education, and the influence of others.

The Three Truths That Eliminate Every Form of Stress

Now, for the good part. The three Universal Truths below are the truthful (unclouded) view of the three Universal Illusions:

1. All things and all people, particularly you, are connected to each other in a continuous stream of energy (love);

2. There is more than enough for everybody, including you, regardless of how much or what specific things (including jobs) others have; and

3. You can never be harmed and you can never die. At some point your body may wear out or stop working due to disease or injury, but the energetic part of you will *always* exist.

A bit earlier I mentioned that Nature does not like a void. Knowing this is particularly important when replacing Illusions with Truth. As you work to dismiss the Illusions causing you Stress and Pain in your life, you will replace it with a better understanding, what is referred to here as a Universal Truth.

You have noticed these three Truths are repeated at the bottom of each Chapter. I want you to repeat them as often as you need until they become part of your core belief system. I want you to *know* them, not just *know of them.*

Three Things to Know:

1. All people and all things, particularly you, are connected to each other in a continuous stream of love;

2. There is more than enough for everybody, including you, regardless of how much or what specific things (including jobs) that other people have; and

3. You can never be harmed and you can never die. At some point your body may wear out or stop working due to disease or injury, yet your energetic you (soul) will always exist.

CHAPTER EIGHT

USING THE STRESS DOMINO TO REMOVE STRESS

CAREY WELLNESS STRESS DOMINO™

The Stress Domino is a tool that helps you identify each of the specific components of your particular Stresses, which you can then address during Meditation. In doing so, you will  release the underlying Fears and, therefore, the source of Stress will be no more. It does this by teaching you the three components needed for Stress to exist and then walks you through switching out the causative components of Stress to a component of Truth it was hiding. This essentially rebuilds or re-wires your conscious and subconscious minds to look at things based on real processing and thinking, not based on incorrect understandings and processes.

Weeds

If you live anywhere where there are weeds, you will certainly have learned by now that if you cut off just the top of the weed or snap the stem by the soil and don't remove the root, your friend the nasty weed is just going to grow right back where it was before. You may *feel* better and *think* your life has improved by seeing the weed gone, but before you know it the weed is back, in spite of all your hard work.

The same is true of Stress. If you do not pull Stress up by the roots and replace it with good clean soil, then with something not nice - your Stress - will return and it will frustrate an otherwise normal, intelligent Human Being. If you've ever done this by having a glass of wine, beer, a cocktail, or by exercising hard, you learned fast that the immediate relief you felt was gone the moment you noticed the new stem pushing up through the earth.

In the following pages you will see earlier information repeated here. This is done this way so that this chapter can stand on its own.

The 3 Threes

There are three sets of things you need to understand in order to attack (or release, depending on your point of view) the main Stress in your life. (By the way, you will not see drinking alcohol or smoking tobacco mentioned anywhere below because it does not do anything positive for you, although I understand their occasional use).

There are three conditions required for Stress to exist. If one or more of them is missing you cannot be Stressed. In many instances, one may *appear* to be missing, but it is there, it is simply misunderstood.

The three conditions for STRESS to exist:

1. There is a THREAT to some aspect of you;
2. A FEAR must be activated in you; and
3. You perceive UNCERTAINTY (real or imagined).

So in English, I want you to observe that, in sum, to be Stressed, a person is exhibiting a reaction, called anxiety, over an expectation. We will use the Stress Domino to gain understanding of the building blocks supporting this, remove the faulty building blocks, and replace them with a sound foundation of Truths.

There are three UNIVERSAL ILLUSIONS which are lies we tell ourselves. Most of these we first meet in childhood and then they are reinforced later in life through jobs, politics, schools, religion, and advertising. Although these are not correct truths, but lies disguising themselves as truths, do not mistake their power and control over everyday life.

The three UNIVERSAL ILLUSIONS are:

1. You are absolutely ALONE and not connected to anybody or anything. You are separated from love;
2. There is a very limited amount of everything that exists; if you do not get it and get it now, there will not be enough left for you; and
3. You can be harmed or killed.

In using the Stress Domino you will learn to recognize these illusions for what they are (bullshit) and you will let them go. But life does not like a void, so we will replace them with the three UNIVERSAL TRUTHS that the ILLUSIONS hide from you.

The three UNIVERSAL TRUTHS are:

1. All people and all things, particularly you, are connected to each other in a continuous stream of energy (LOVE);
2. There is more than enough for everybody, including you, regardless of how much or what specific things (including jobs) that other people have; and
3. You can never be harmed and you can never die. At some point your body may wear out or stop working due to disease or injury, yet your energetic you will always exist. Many people refer to the energetic you as a soul.

Completing Your Stress Domino Chart

On the next page is the Stress Domino chart. (There is another copy of it in the Appendix, Section J).

We are going to tie together everything we just learned, so here are the steps to completing your own Stress Domino chart:

*   Line 1. Put in a STRESS in your life, a major one and/or one you've experienced recently (a recent one can be a strong hint about what area to work on now).
*   Line 2. Feel and think about what the underlying FEAR may be. Write that here.

- Line 3. FEARS flow from misunderstandings, which we call ILLUSIONS. Put an "X" in Line 3 that causes the FEAR from Line 2.
- Line 4. The Universe does not like a vacuum. Put an "X" next to the TRUTH in Line 4 that best replaces the ILLUSION from Line 3.

Once you have done this, you should have a much better under-standing, and soon feeling, about the cause of the Stress and lack of any need for it. Have you ever heard the expression "The Truth shall set you free"? It's the very same thing. If you are not afraid of anything, then you would not be concerned about any-one knowing any detail of you, right? Most of us won't get to 100% Fear-free by the end of our lifetimes, but we don't have to, to enjoy a significantly Stress-free life.

	CAREY Wellness Stress Domino™ 				
	Underlying Function	**A**	**B**	**C**	**Example**
1	Stress/ Stressful Situation	_____	_____	_____	Rejection at asking someone out on a date
2	Underlying Fear	_____	_____	_____	I am not enough; people will laugh at me
3	Three Universal Illusions	Match the FEAR in #2 with the underlying ILLUSION that supports it. Mark each that applies to each fear. There are sometimes more than one, rarely all three, and usually if there are 2 or more, one ILLUSION is dominant by a lot.			
	Illusion 1	_____	_____	_____	Yes, mostly
	Illusion 2	_____	_____	_____	Yes, partially
	Illusion 3	_____	_____	_____	No
4	Three Universal Truths	Match the ILLUSION above with the TRUTH the ILLUSION is hiding. As with ILLUSIONS, more than one may apply, but rarely three, and there is usually a dominant one.			
	Truth 1	_____	_____	_____	Yes, mostly
	Truth 2	_____	_____	_____	Yes, partially
	Truth 3	_____	_____	_____	No

Consider this: The TRUTHS in #4 are covered up by the ILLUSIONS in #3, which cause the FEARS in #2, which when ACTIVATED, cause the STRESS in #1.

When you replace the ILLUSIONS in #3 with the TRUTHS in #4, the Fears in #2 and the STRESSES in #1 will fall down around you, JUST LIKE DOMINOS!

Instructions to Completing the Table:

- Line 1. Put in a STRESS in your life, a major one and/or ones you've experienced recently (A recent one can be a strong hint about what area to work on now.)

- Line 2. Feel and think about what the underlying FEAR may be. Write this here.

- Line 3. FEARS flow from misunderstandings which we call ILLUSIONS. Put an "X" next to the Illusion in Line 3 that causes the FEAR from Line 2.

- Line 4. The Universe does not like a vacuum. Put an "X" next to the TRUTH in Line 4 that best replaces the ILLUSION from Line 3.

Meditation Using the Stress Domino to Release Stress

We will go through a Guided Meditation to eliminate Stress, much as we do any other Guided Meditation, but we will have the advantage of bringing a detailed understanding of the Stress and how to relieve it.

1. <u>Find your place to Meditate.</u> Your Meditation sweet spot or staged space.

2. Get comfortable and relax your body. Think of your body as a stick of butter, getting a gentle massage from the bottom of your feet up to the top of your head (don't forget your ears). As the massage moves up from one part of your body to the next, your body melts into nothing, like a warm stick of butter.

    Breathe in and out, focusing on your breath. Don't breathe harder, just a second or two longer. Equal breath in, hold equally, equal breath out.

3. Relax and quiet your mind. Let any thoughts gently pass by, without judgment or concern. Place persistent or particularly annoying thoughts into your Distraction Box.

    Breathe in and out, focusing on your breath. Don't breathe harder, just a second or two longer. Equal breath in, hold equally, equal breath out.

    Use your mantra if you wish. It can be as simple as counting from 1 to 10 and, without breaking stride, continue counting from 1 to 10 again, in a loop. I use a slowly rotating water-wheel (in my mind) to help me stay on count.

4. Set an intention to find and expand your understanding of the Stress you are exploring today, and how to best release it.

5. Consider how Stress affects your Inner Life. You are not your body and you are not your mind. You are something much greater and you contain great wisdom. You have been offered the chance to live inside your body while you walk upon the Earth. How will you benefit

your body today so that it will not be hurt further by your Stress?

a) Sense where in your body your Stress exists. You may perceive more than one area, so check around and make sure you are working with the Stress to be addressed today. We will refer to it as the Alpha Stress.

b) Once you locate the Alpha Stress, consider its shape. Its size. Its density. Its color. Its temperature.

c) Ask Alpha Stress what caused it to be created. What event or experience brought it to be.

d) Ask how the Alpha Stress feels when it is activated.

e) Visualize and feel great love and appreciation for the Alpha Stress, as the event or experience is likely to have been quite unpleasant.

f) Consider what happened to cause the Stress. Is that situation relevant to today? If not, explain that you do not live in those circumstances and that such an event will not happen again. You will be certain to make sure of it.

g) If the situation is relevant today, explain what you learned about the Stress-Fear-Illusion-Truth relationship from the Domino. Dialogue with the Stress the clear understanding that you've now learned. Explain that the Truth will protect it from the Illusion and that you will too.

h) In your mind - look up and see a bright - but not blinding light. Visualize and feel the Stress-Fear-Illusion moving into the light to be taken back to its source.

i) Replace the area where the Alpha Stress existed with the appropriate Truth. What is the shape of the new Truth? Its size. Its density. Its color. Its temperature. Ask your Higher Guidance for a symbol to lock-in the new inner-strength and imprint it upon the new feeling.

j) Be with this for 8 minutes.

k) Know that a mostly Stress-free life is naturally intended for you. This does not mean you won't find challenges and occasionally deal with life's speed bumps, but it *does mean* you are not meant to exist in fear.

l) Be still with what you - all of you - now feels. Now understand. It is perfection. It is pure. It is joy.

6. Give thanks and return from your Meditation slowly.

Three Things to Know:

1. All people and all things, particularly you, are connected to each other in a continuous stream of love;

2. There is more than enough for everybody, including you, regardless of how much or what specific things (including jobs) that other people have; and

3. You can never be harmed and you can never die. At some point your body may wear out or stop working due to disease or injury, yet your energetic you (soul) will always exist.

PART THREE - DEEP DIVE/ADVANCED MEDITATION TECHNIQUES USING INNER ESSENCES TO ELIMINATE STRESS *AND* EMOTIONAL BLOCKS, SOLVE PROBLEMS, INCREASE CREATIVITY, AND SOLVE MANY OTHER CHALLENGES (A GLOBAL ACCESS MEDITATION METHOD)

CHAPTER NINE

ACCESSING YOUR INNER INTELLIGENCE: USING INNER ESSENCES TO ELIMINATE STRESS AND EMOTIONAL BLOCKS, SOLVE PROBLEMS, INCREASE CREATIVITY, AND SOLVE MANY OTHER CHALLENGES

"The inner condition creates the external circumstance."
~ Harvey Grady

Your Inner Essences – Your Inner Intelligence

Remember, I said it was getting interesting? Trust me, it's going to get *really* interesting - right now as this chapter contains 98% of the information in the book.

I don't know about you, but I'll bet a lot of people are like me in that I believe there are varying feelings within myself. Some days, for instance, when I practice Taekwondo, I feel really strong and masculine. But then an hour later I am home and am greeted by our new puppy, Gigi, and my heart just explodes in my chest. At these times I am feeling much more feminine (but still being a male).

These varied feelings are pretty understandable to me, but sometimes I get a little embarrassed by them because I have this little Mind Chatter voice, *that we all have*, in the back of my mind, that says things like: "You can't, you're not good enough; You're stupid; Don't do that or people are really going to laugh at you," and blah, blah, blah. It was like there was some other part of me that was judging my every move every time I went to do something big or fun with my life (which were different things to me). And the darn thing kept telling me *not* to do it and gave me all sorts of reasons not to do it. It told me as a guy I shouldn't find Gigi adorable. And the problem was, the Mind Chatter sounded smart!

Back in the 1990s, it became common to refer to a person's "Inner Child." There was even a comedian with a joke that went, "I have so many Inner Children that I need an Inner Mini-Van!" (I love this joke, even today!) Maybe this is why Chrysler invented the minivan after all. Does anyone personally know Lee Iacocca to find out?

The problem was, although I could trace some of my fears back to childhood, many of my Fears seemed to be about things adults deal with every day (e.g., potential loss of a job, divorce, raising children properly, illnesses, and the like).

My solution to this quandary was to use a view of my subconscious that could easily be worked with and included things that made sense to me like male, female, and judgment. I found this in Inner Essences.

Inner Essences

Instead of Inner Children, Inner Mini-Vans, and annoying noise in my mind, the framework here includes Inner Essences that deal with all my issues and concerns, whether from my childhood, my teenage years, or more often than not, what I am working through right now. **Inner Essence Meditation gives you direct access to your Inner Intelligence.**

The Inner Essences are our internal storage devices that harbor emotions (good or bad) and past experiences (also, good or bad). But it is important to know that they can be dialogued with as if they are also internal intelligences. This means we can dialogue with them to figure out problems. They are the subconscious aspects of ourselves. These are adult aspects of ourselves, not immature, child-like aspects of our subconscious mind. Interact with them respectfully. *It would not be inaccurate to consider the Inner Essence Model as simply a language that enhances your ability to dialogue with your subconscious.*

> Key Note: My solution to this quandary was to use a view of my subconscious that could easily be worked with and included things that made sense to me.

> Key Note: The Inner Essences are our internal storage devices that harbor emotions and past experiences. But it is important to know that they are also internal intelligences. This means we can dialogue with them to figure out and work through our problems.

Inner Essences is a model that shows the inside or subconscious aspects of ourselves. It includes the relationships between Inner,

Outer, and Higher Essences. These are adult aspects of ourselves – not immature remnants of childhood, although those remnants are certainly there within the Essences.

> Key Note: Inner Essences is a model that shows the inside or subconscious aspects of ourselves. It is not ultimate Truth, but it is extremely effective at producing needed changes in peoples' lives quickly and permanently.

> Key Note: It would not be inaccurate to consider the Inner Essence Model as simply a language that enhances your ability to dialogue with your subconscious.

Once you become adept at the framework of Inner Essences, jump to Appendix I and do the Inner Essence Meditation.

(See the next page for a graphic of the Inner Essences Model, Figure 1).

Figure One. Inner Essences

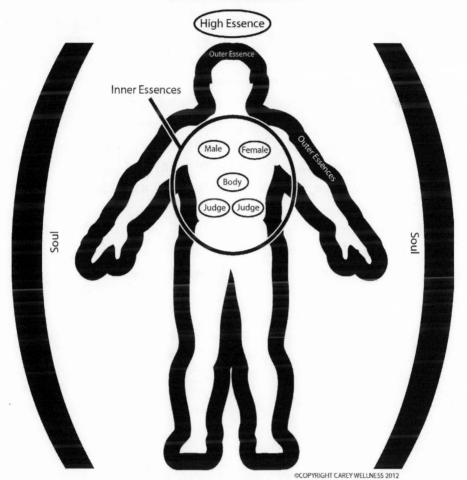

©COPYRIGHT CAREY WELLNESS 2012

At first glance, the Inner Essences model has a number of moving parts and may seem complicated, but as each part is defined, I'll bet you will recognize what you already know. Maybe you are already having a good communication with *your* Inner Essences.

Here's the concept: We are Outer Essences and within us are Inner Essences that represent Archetypes (it's worth doing a search on this term). We are guided/assisted by a Higher Essence (Advanced Being) that is of greater development than us. All of which is cradled within the loving energy egg of the soul. (By the way, I use the term "soul" in energetic terms and do not wish it to be confused with any religious term; it is not used that way here).

The term Personality means "you and all that is you," as shown in the Inner Essences model. Another way to look at it is: Your "Personality" = Inner Essences + Outer Essences + High Essence.

Key Note: Your "Personality" = Inner Essences + Outer Essences + High Essence.

Let's look at each Essence:

Inner Essences ("Lower Essences"):

1. Male Essence - the "male" energy / consciousness, often associated with power

2. Female Essence - the "female" energy / consciousness, often associated with love

3. Body Essence - the energy / consciousness that cares for the physical body

4. Judge Essence M - the description will be discussed in advanced material; often much fear resides here (a "shadow" aspect of your Personality)

5. Judge Essence A - the description will be discussed in advanced material; often much fear resides here (a "shadow" aspect of your Personality)

When working with the paradigm of Past Lives and Inner Essences, which is an extremely effective way to work through "issues" in your life, Past Life experiences are the experience of the Male and Female Inner Essences, but not of you, the Outer Essence.

Outer Essence:

6. Outer Essence. That's you and me. When we are thinking and walking and visualizing and working in and working out, that's what you think of as you and what I think of as me. Most often thought of as your mind, but it is more than that and somewhat separate.

Higher Essence:

7. Higher Essence. This is an energy/consciousness that is an Advanced Being which has advanced Knowledge, advanced Wisdom, and guides us in our lives.

Soul:

8. Soul Essence. The energy / consciousness that envelopes a Personality and is its direct connection to all other things. (This definition is improved upon in advanced studies). The Human Personality exists entirely within the energetic egg of the energetic soul.

Eight aspects is a lot to work with and does not help beginning Meditators to Meditate. In fact, it would drive many people crazy. In this book we will work with your two primary Inner Essences: your Male Essence and your Female Essence. We are only going to work with them in *Chasin' Meditation*. (Dialoging with the other Essences is a Deep Dive / Advanced Topic).

When you have established a working relationship with your Male Essence (1) and your Female Essence (2), you will be 95% on your way to removing many barriers in your life, in many instances. You will be removing one barrier at a time, but it may only take weeks or *days* using the Inner Essence model. Once these barriers are removed, you will be exploring and growing, not just working through difficulties.

Working with the other Essences is an even more Advanced topic and usually is best addressed after establishing a good working relationship with your Male and Female Essences.

Key Note: When you have established a working relationship with your Male Essence (1) and your Female Essence (2), you will be 95% on your way to removing the barriers in your life, in many instances. You will be removing one barrier at a time, but it may only take weeks or *days* using the Inner Essence model. Once these barriers are removed, you will be exploring and growing, not just working through difficulties.

Another feature of the Male and Female Essences is they have primary skill sets, or styles of consciousness, built into them. They are:

1. Outerspacial – meaning intelligence;
2. Angelic – meaning altruistic helping of others;
3. Devic – meaning deep connection with Nature; and
4. Elemental – meaning focus on creature comforts such as eating, resting, exercising, and sex

Most of the Male and Female Essences will have just one of these primary skill sets. Some people have Inner Essences with more than one primary skill set, like me, but that is a Deep Dive/ Advanced Topic.

The most important thing for you to know about this aspect of your Inner Essences is that these skill sets will represent significant preferences to them. For example, if you have Inner Essences with an Angelic and a Devic skill set, but you are a jerk living in a dirty, congested city, you will likely have significant challenges in your life relative to these areas. Meaning, even though you are a jerk, it is not necessarily going to feel good when you are being a jerk. And if you live in a dirty city, you will be challenged to enjoy it.

You may find, upon dialoguing with your Inner Essences, that one is a flower child from the 70's, as pictured above, or at least they *think* they are. Nonetheless, being a flower child may be part of who you are. Part of your Inner Being. Well, depending on how you look at it, you can think being a flower child is pretty cool or pretty uncool. The smartest thing you can do, as well as the best thing you can do, is **to appreciate, respect, and love your Inner Essences and all their preferences.** The good, the bad, the ugly, and trust me, there is going to be bad and there is going to be ugly.

For the bad and ugly parts, you do not want to emulate those preferences or act out on them of course, but you do want to acknowledge them as legitimate experiences and preferences. (Dialoging on how to work through the ugly and bad, if still active, is a Deep Dive topic, but essentially, the dialogue focuses on a clear understanding of circumstances and connection with all others).

When we ignore our inner preferences, there will be resistance. In Meditation workshops I teach students how to create agreements with their Inner Essences to accommodate their preferences and in by doing so, accelerating their ability to create the life they desire.

Key Note: The most important thing for you to know about this aspect of your Inner Essences is that these skill sets will represent significant preferences to them.

Dealing with Stress Using Inner Essences

Remember that Stress is a *threat* to some aspect to you. It is living in the presence of an Active Fear. The resulting Active Fear is a reaction, often from your subconscious mind, that you are going to do something it really doesn't want you to do or that something is going to happen to you that it *really* doesn't want to happen to you.

If we eliminate your Fear(s), Stress **cannot** occur.

> Key Note: If we eliminate your Fear(s), Stress **cannot** occur.

The subconscious aspects of you that hold and release Fear are your Inner Essences: your Male, Female, and Judge Essences (not so much with the Body Essence). Think and work with your underlying Fears and Stress this way. When you dialogue with an Inner Essence with the approach that it "owns" the Fear that is causing you Stress, it will be much easier for you to eliminate the Fear and the Stress.

> Key Note: Stress is living in the presence of a perceived threat to some aspect (aka Essence) of you. Your Fears are your (usually subconscious) reaction/conclusion to a potential outcome or event, real or perceived. The reaction is ALWAYS with one or more Inner Essences.

> **Key Note: Learn to work with Stress in this way, and *ALL* the barriers in your life will fall down around you.**

Each and every Fear is a reaction to a potential outcome, real or perceived. Let's look at an example - first a fictitious one - and then I will share one of my own personal experiences.

Example: You are afraid of crossing a very busy street. What's the Fear?

> Answer. Your Body Essence is fearful of it suffering enormous trauma and perhaps death.

Makes sense, right? You should be pretty glad to have this Fear, because if you didn't, you'd be road kill, right? (That would be a bad day). Everybody knows not to cross a busy street, so let's look at something most of us were not taught to deal with.

A Very Personal Example:

I got divorced in the mid-1990s and found myself wanting to date and perhaps remarry (which I did, to great lady, Lisa "Las Vegas"). One problem: *I was too scared to ask a woman out on a date.* Ridiculous, stupid, impossible? Maybe. A more compassionate view would be embarrassing and painful. And painful it was. Here I was, 38 years old, and I could *not* ask a woman out on a date.

So knowing what you just learned, what would you do? Right, I got into a Meditative state, approached my Inner Essences, and asked which one contained the Fear of asking a woman out on a date.

The Male Essence said it was with him. I asked him what happened to give him that fear. Instantly, and I mean instantly, I was in a High Definition video clip of a summer dance in 1930s rural Kansas (a Midwestern state in the US); there "he" was, asking a girl to dance. She laughed at him, out loud in front of all her friends and some of his. He was shameful and *thoroughly* embarrassed. It left him hurting enormously.

There are many things I could have communicated to him: shame, hurt, anger, but knowing that I too have been in embarrassing situations, I energetically visualized completely surrounding him with love, compassion, and appreciation, and I felt the warmth of my heart envelop him. I shared with him that I had compassion for him on that very hard night back in Kansas; that I respected what he had experienced and invited him to grow from it, by moving beyond it, which I showed him how to do.

Using Inner Essences to Eliminate Emotional Blocks, Solve Problems, and Increase Creativity, and Solve Other Challenges

Simply recognizing and acknowledging Stresses, Fears, and preferences will go a very long way to releasing their grip on you. People *and* Inner Essences seek validation. And after all, your Inner Essences are you.

They say in politics that most loud opposition is simply a disguise for someone saying: "Why didn't you ask me!?" Once we understand our thoughts and emotions are recognized and considered valid by others, we no longer dig ourselves in around pointing them out. (Chew on this for a few days. Notice the areas where you dig yourself into a hole or position and won't come out, even though you *know* it does not make sense.)

Key Note: Simply recognizing and acknowledging Stresses, Fears, and preferences will go a very long way to releasing their grip on you. People *and* Inner Essences seek validation.

Key Note: You must completely embrace, accept, and love each and every thing you are, regardless of how bad, or even horrible, it may be to you. If you do not accept, love and appreciate fully all the bad things "you" and your Inner Essences experienced/did, you may not get past them and these experiences will keep you anchored in your problems like a lead ball.

Key Note: You must first come to acceptance with your Inner Essences before you can work directly with your Higher Essence. This is reflected in the Hawaiian Huna tradition which says you must go down before you go up. This is what they mean.

Key Note: Learn to work with Stress in this way, and *ALL* of the barriers in your life will fall down around you.

I want to share with you a few more things.

Information Delivery

Because you are in an Expanded State of Awareness during Meditation, information comes at a higher level; and higher level always means more efficiently and more effectively. Information often comes in full or short or short answers, but those are mostly "heard." But not heard in the traditional way, with audio. The sentence or a short sentence will be perceived as a thought.

There are also Thought Balls, which I call Information Infusions. These are much like one large, complete and unified set of information passing to you in a moment. So, for example, if in an Advanced Meditation you asked the question, "What is Love," it is quite possible that you will perceive it coming and then in a moment, a ball of knowledge will have engulfed you and in that moment you will have a complete understanding of Love. As you are in this Infusion, you can look around at different aspects of Love and see the details. (Note that even though the amount of information may be quite large, in my experience the information comes to you without the perception of force, meaning at one moment you don't know and the next moment you know a lot, but you have not been slammed. Make sense? It will.)

Spock's Brain

If you are a Trekky or know a Trekky, remember the episode or ask your friend to tell you about the episode called "Spock's Brain." (It originally aired on September 20, 1968; I saw it 10 years later). Without all the lead up, in short, Bones needed to understand the anatomy of Spock's brain so he could put it back into Spock's head. He and Spock did the Vulcan Mind Meld, and Bones instantly got an Information Infusion of Spock's brain's anatomy and instantly knew 100% of everything there was to know of it. Also, the complexity of the brain's reattachment became clear and completely uncomplicated.

The knowledge of existence of a Thought Ball, which I refer to as an Information Infusion, is where, I suspect, the writers of Star Trek derived the concept.

A Note of Caution

When you work with advanced Meditation techniques you can be delving into some of the darker areas of yourself. There are some influences that do not want you there.

If you get what sounds like bad information from an Inner Essence or your Higher Essence, ask, "Are you my Inner Essence / Higher Essence?" If the answer is "No," tell them to go away and never bother you again. (Trust me on this one, please.)

I personally know people who have listened to bad information and subsequently made really bad decisions in their life. If you get information in a Meditation that tells you that should swim the English Channel but you don't know how to swim, don't do it. If you get information that says you should fly off the tallest building, but you weren't born with wings, don't do it. Anything that doesn't pass the sniff test or a few days reflection, just don't do it.

Not everything you receive in Meditation will be received clearly or interpreted correctly. If it sounds ridiculous, consider it ridiculous and try again, or at least tread lightly.

How to Use Inner Essences to Eliminate Stress and Emotional Blocks, Solve Problems, Increase Creativity, and Solve Other Challenges

The process is simple and it is relatively the same regardless of what you are wanting to get done. I mentioned in the beginning of the book that you can achieve results with the following concerns using Inner Essence Meditation™:

- Stress Elimination
- Problem Solving in Business
- Problem Solving in Life
- Trauma and Grief Release
- Memory Improvement
- Life Planning
- Choice Analysis
- Connection with Higher Consciousness
- And about 10,000 additional, even more fascinating things

So how does this work? The IE Model states that the Male and Female essences have one or more of four primary skill sets or traits as mentioned earlier. Here are additional characteristics:

- They house the Fears that cause you Stress
- They have traits such as intelligence (Outerspacial) and/or creativity that can help you solve problems
- They affect the effectiveness of your five senses

- They house experiences that have caused trauma and/or grief in your life
- They affect your ability to remember
- They have desires for you during your lifetime and can help you achieve yours by bringing to you people and resources who can help you
- It is essential to have a good rapport with them before you can have a clear dialogue with your High Essence

So how do they help you with these areas of your life? You establish a good working relationship with them through dialogue, accept and understand their experiences, and help them with their preferences. You do this through consistent dialogue with them, asking for their assistance, and offering your assistance in return. Period.

No, "yeah, but's." Have no resistance to moving through uncomfortable challenges. In fact, my brother Kevin, who is a Federal Judge, was once asked what he did to advance his career so successfully. His answer: "I always run *toward* challenges, not away."

So back to IE Meditation. Simply do it. Dialogue, converse, agree, disagree, test, fail, succeed, fail again, succeed better. When I teach IE Meditation the introductions takes less than 60 minutes and then I take students through Meditation after Meditation after Meditation. It is no different than riding a bike. You or I could lecture someone about it all day long, day in and day out, but the real learning starts the moment our student gets onto the bike. Right?

A Real Life Example Using
IE's to Solve a Business Problem

This is a true story. I was in the corporate world, lastly, as a VP of Underwriting for a Fortune 500 insurance company with a well-recognized name, Aetna. I had worked for a smaller regional company for 3 years before it was bought by Aetna. When we were purchased I applied for one of 6 or 7 VP of Underwriting slots and got it. Those are very big positions in insurance companies and *all* insurance companies live or die based on the performance of their underwriters. So I was really excited to have the opportunity.

Large group underwriters need a good dose of both mathematical ability and business sense. I had both of these which made me a natural for the position. But, there were people who had more mathematical ability than me, such as Actuaries. Well just a few weeks into the new job, I needed to be on a conference call to price out a very large and important group we were bidding on. Mike, the company President, and several other very high ups were on the call. This was my first "performance" with Mike on the phone in the new organization. Cool, I had no problem with that and everything went well until we got about 12 minutes into the call. We were all in sync as to what the company should do and we were excited about the opportunity as it would be a big win.

Then bam! Someone asked a question *well outside of my mathematical ability*. We are talking major Stress! The question was something like this (I do not recall the exact details.): In the pricing we were going for a profit pricing of, say, 85 for instance. The bam question someone asked was, "Well if we do such and such, what would the 85 turn into?" Reasonable question. Normal question. Important question. The only problem was, I HAD NO IDEA HOW TO DO THE MATH AND THERE WAS NO ONE IN OR NEAR MY OFFICE WHO COULD HELP ME.

Have you ever been in a situation so Stressful that time stops, sound stops, and you have NO IDEA what to do next? You have? That was ME, Mr. Vice President of Underwriting!

So you are thinking by now that I was toast. I wasn't. I had built such a successful relationship with my Male Essence, the more mathematical of my two IE's, that I quickly snapped into a Meditative state (notice I did not have to relax my body or quiet my mind) and asked him for help. INSTANTLY a formula appeared in my mind. I applied it to the question at hand, and gave the answer to Mike: 92 (or some such number). Mike said: "I'm good with that. Any objections?" None came back. Mike said: "Chase, will you redo the numbers and get them distributed this afternoon?" I said: "Mike, you bet."

I hung up and then ran as fast as I could to the Actuary's office (Pam), sweat pouring off my forehead, stopped short of her office, collected myself, and casually walked in to say hi. She asked about the call, and I casually threw out the formula I had used and asked her if she would have used the same. She said: "Yes, why?" My response: "Oh, I dunno know, just wondering." I thanked her, headed back to my office, wiped my forehead, and got back to work revising the exhibits.

Okay, I was having some fun with you on the above. The facts are all true but although anxious, I was not sweating or panicking…BECAUSE of the relationship I knew I had with my Inner Essences. In many ways people viewed my Meditation experience as an unfair advantage in the corporate world, but I viewed it as a no brainer. We expect people that work out to win marathons and we expect those that don't, to not win. Why shouldn't we expect better business skill and performance from those who Meditate versus those who don't?

Three Things to Know:

1. All people and all things, particularly you, are connected to each other in a continuous stream of love;

2. There is more than enough for everybody, including you, regardless of how much or what specific things (including jobs) that other people have; and

3. You can never be harmed and you can never die. At some point your body may wear out or stop working due to disease or injury, yet your energetic you (soul) will always exist.

CHAPTER TEN

RESOURCES

You may reach each of these and other links at
www.CareyWellness.com/Resources

Meditation

CAREY Wellness – Speaking and Teaching
Meditation for Corporations – Professional
Meditation and Executive Meditation –
www.CareyWellness.com

McLean Meditation Institute, SEED
Meditation Instructors – www.sedona-
meditation.com/meditationteachers.htm

The Monroe Institute (Technology Assisted Meditation – CD's,
books, and more) - www.MonroeInstitute.org

National Institutes of Health - www.ncam.NIH.gov/health/meditation

Holistic, Emotional, Mental, and Energy Healing

Edgar Cayce Institute (Holistic, etc.) - www.EdgarCayce.org

Asha Lightbearer – Prosperity for Women and Direct Readings – www.AshaLightbearer.com

Carolyn Myss (Energy, etc.-Myss is pronounced "Mace") - www.Myss.com

Catherine P. Perry, M.Ed, DD (Intuitive Spiritual Healer, Author, Motivational Speaker, Coach) - www.CatherinePPerry.net

Doreen Virtue, Angel Therapy - www.AngelTherapy.com

Executive, Professional, Team, and Corporate Coaching at a High Levels, Visionary

Kathryn Small – www.ProfoundImpact.ca

Physical Health and Fitness

Cathryn Marshall – www.SimplyCathryn.com

Law of Attraction

Abraham-Hicks - www.Abraham-Hicks.com

Self Help

InnerTalk (CDs for subconscious reprogramming) - www.InnerTalk.com

Norm Shealy, MD (Self-Help) - www.NormShealy.com

Shamanism

Hank Wesselmen (Remarkable books, workshops, and more) - www.SharedWisdom.com

Imprinting Archetypes Into Water
(THIS IS A MUST READ)

Water Geometry by Masaru Emoto - www.Masaru-Emoto.net

ABOUT C. CHASE CAREY, MBA

Chase comes from Corporate America, having spent 20 years in significant positions with health insurance and consulting companies. In 1998, as a VP of Underwriting for Aetna, Inc., he sent an email to the Chief Medical Officer and several other Senior Executives he worked with, telling them of the benefits of meditation and other Complementary and Alternative Medicine (CAM) techniques. He offered to help the company become a major force in bringing these techniques to the health insurance industry and the people it took care of. Two days later he received a courteous reply admitting it all made sense but that he was simply "too far ahead of them".

In the 1990s, Chase's Meditation training work began at The Monroe Institute in Virginia. There, they use patented audio technology to move students into deep states of Meditation within minutes of arriving. He participated in six week-long programs, which are 24/7 immersions into deep Meditation using Guided exploration.

The training at TMI enabled him to re-enter any number of Meditative states, near instantaneously, at will, anywhere, anytime, including while at work solving complex business problems as a career Insurance Executive. He can teach you to do this, too.

Chase then trained with an advanced Teacher in Sedona, AZ, for 2+ years, with Karen Malik, MA, one of the Founding Trainers of The Monroe Institute, and other reputable organizations.

In his first 10 years of Meditative work, he personally Meditated for over 1,500 hours, including an hour in the Kingschamber of the Great Pyramid, in Gaza, Egypt.

Chase is certified as a Meditation Teacher, Reiki Master, Jin Shin Jyutsu Practitioner, and Personal Self Integration Teacher, where he helps students dialogue with their Inner Essences.

His *real* Certification is that most of the illnesses and distractions that plagued him for so long are now gone. And consider this: during the time he had significant health issues he continued to be a father, a husband, an active member of his community, and yes, a Corporate Athlete.

In addition to teaching the SEED Meditation, he also teaches his personally developed Inner Essence Meditation™, Professional Meditation™, and Stress Domino Stress-Release Meditations™ (these meditations work like nothing you've ever experienced before!)

He has an advanced business degree from Villanova University (MBA) and an undergraduate degree (BS) from Penn State. He is a certified Master Scuba Diver, active pistol and rifle enthusiast, hiker, a student of Taekwondo, loves to travel, and has a particular fondness for the Southwest of the United States.

He has a fun side which is demonstrated by his appearances as the GEICO Gecko, and his appearances as an Extra in TV and movies, such as Drop Dead Diva, Necessary Roughness, and the A&E production of COMA. Life is so much more fun dressed as the Gecko!

He wishes to share what he has learned so, you too, can benefit from his experiences. Let him help you.

C. Chase Carey, MBA
O 770.751.6700
Info@CareyWellness
www.CareyWellness.com

APPENDIX

A. DAILY MEDITATION

1. Find your place to Meditate. Your Meditation sweet spot or staged space.

2. Get comfortable and relax your body. Roll around on your hip bones, rotate your shoulders, mover your fingers and toes, and find your comfort zone. Think of your body as a stick of butter, getting a gentle massage from the bottom of your feet up to the top of your head (don't forget your ears). As the massage moves up from one part of your body to the next, your body melts into nothing, like a warm stick of butter.

3. Breathe in and out, focusing on your breath. Don't breathe harder, just a second or two longer. Equal breath in, hold equally, equal breath out.

4. Relax and quiet your mind. Let any thoughts gently pass by, without judgment or concern. Place persistent or particularly annoying thoughts into your Distraction Box.

    Breathe in and out, focusing on your breath. Don't breathe harder, just a second or two longer. Equal breath in, hold equally, equal breath out.

    Use your mantra if you wish. It can be as simple as counting from 1 - 10 and, without breaking stride, continue counting from 1 - 10 again, in a loop. I use a slowly rotating water-wheel (in my mind) to help me stay on count.

5. Set an intention if you wish. For daily Meditation, these are very helpful: "to move effortlessly through the Stress

of the day; "to recognize my connection with the loving dance of life; "to love my body, mind, heart and the health they bring to me."

6. For an immediate need or remedy to an urgent challenge, connect with your Inner Essence or Higher Guidance.

7. Give thanks and return from your Meditation slowly.

8. Either do this Meditation for 20 minutes twice a day or for 35-40 minutes once a day. You can miss a day or two without any concern, just like you may miss a day or two of exercise to allow for your healing and rebalance.

B. QUICK RESET MEDITATION TO RELEASE IMMEDITATE STRESS

Use the Quick Reset Meditation when you are about to enter into a very Stressful situation: a business meeting, a first date, a car accident, a job interview, or an audition. You can cut this Meditation out of the sheet and fold it into your wallet for fast reference.

1. Squiggle your body to get it comfortable.

2. Breathe in and out, 5-8 times. Don't breathe harder, but for 2-4 seconds longer than normal. Equal breath in, hold equally, equal breath out. Less if it causes any dizziness.

3. Quiet your mind. Let distracting thoughts pass, and repeat in your mind or aloud:

   • I am perfectly complete and exactly what is needed

   • I am cherished and loved more than words can ever tell me

   • I am the right person, at the right place, at the right time

Discomfort means you are growing, and life *loves* growth. Your Soul loves growth.

4. Breathe in and out, 5-8 times. Don't breathe harder, but for 2-4 seconds longer than normal. Equal breath in, hold equally, equal breath out. Less if it causes any dizziness.

5. Return to you, bringing all of you to the opportunity at hand. Shine, flourish, and rejoice.

C. BODY AWARENESS (RELAXATION) MEDITATION

1. <u>Find your place to Meditate.</u> Your Meditation sweet spot or staged space.

2. <u>Get comfortable and relax your body.</u> Roll around on your hip bones, rotate your shoulders, move your fingers and toes, and find your comfort zone. Think of your body as a stick of butter, getting a gentle massage from the bottom of your feet up to the top of your head (don't forget your ears). As the massage moves up from one part of your body to the next, your body melts into nothing, like a warm stick of butter.

   <u>Breathe in and out</u>, focusing on your breath. Don't breathe harder, just a second or two longer. Equal breath in, hold equally, equal breath out.

3. <u>Relax and quiet your mind.</u> Let any thoughts gently pass by, without judgment or concern. Place persistent or particularly annoying thoughts into your Distraction Box.

   <u>Breathe in and out</u>, focusing on your breath. Don't breathe harder, just a second or two longer. Equal breath in, hold equally, equal breath out.

   <u>Use your mantra if you wish.</u> It can be as simple as counting from 1 - 10 and without breaking stride, continue counting from 1 - 10 again, in a loop. I use a slowly rotating water-wheel (in my mind) to help me stay on count.

4. Set an intention to find and remove impurities and dysfunctions in your physical and energetic bodies.

5. Envision a high gloss surgical stainless steel screen just above your head.

    It can be a round screen, horizontal, above you.

    a   Lower the screen slowly through your body, starting at the head and working down to the feet

    b   The screen traps all toxins, impurities, imperfections, and black emotions that exist in your body

    c   As the screen passes down through your body, the screen preserves your healthy radiating energetic bodies and the flesh and bone of your physical body, passing through them. The screen catches and pushes down and out of your body the toxins, impurities, imperfections, and black emotions

    d   Run this through your whole being

    e   When you get to the end, wrap all the eliminations in white light and return them to their source to be used for Nature's highest good. Love them and send them away.

    f   Feel your bodies awash in a cool stream of spring water, as they fill you from head to foot.

6. Give thanks and return from your Meditation slowly.

D. FORGIVENESS MEDITATION

1. Find your place to Meditate. Your Meditation sweet spot or staged space.

2. Get comfortable and relax your body. Roll around on your hip bones, rotate your shoulders, mover your fingers and toes, and find your comfort zone. Think of your body as a stick of butter, getting a gentle massage from the bottom of your feet up to the top of your head (don't forget your ears). As the massage moves up from one part of your body to the next, your body melts into nothing, like a warm stick of butter.

   Breathe in and out, focusing on your breath. Don't breathe harder, just a second or two longer. Equal breath in, hold equally, equal breath out.

3. Relax and quiet your mind. Let any thoughts gently pass by, without judgment or concern. Place persistent or particularly annoying thoughts into your Distraction Box.

   Breathe in and out, focusing on your breath. Don't breathe harder, just a second or two longer. Equal breath in, hold equally, equal breath out.

   Use your mantra if you wish. It can be as simple as counting from 1 - 10 and without breaking stride, continue counting from 1 - 10 again, in a loop. I use a slowly rotating water-wheel (in my mind) to help me stay on count.

4. Set an intention to find and release anger and resentment toward specific people and events that hold you back in your life.

5. Consider two people or events that caused you harm in your life and one future event that will be wonderful. We will focus on each one separately. It can be a parent, a sibling, a school mate, a teacher, a neighbor, a boss, etc. The person can be alive or dead. The event can be past, present, or future, although it is best to start with past events and work forward.

   a) [Assume this is a HARMFUL PERSON]. Visualize the person. Invite them into your space and ask that they connect with you.

   b) Consider what harm they caused you.

   c) Feel how you felt in the days after that harm: Hurt, anger, violation, desertion, terror. Accept all emotions.

   d) Envision and feel yourself projecting love to them. See its brightness, feel its warmth, know its beauty.

   e) See God consciousness enveloping the person with love and appreciation.

   f) Understand, at your very core, the love of this person and that they are divinity.

   g) Give thanks to the person and take leave of them.

h) [Assume this is a HARMFUL EVENT]. Remember back to the event. Consider who you were and what you were like.

i) Invite the event into your space and ask that it connect with you.

j) Consider what harm the event caused you.

k) Feel how you felt in the days after that harm. Hurt, anger, violation, desertion, terror.....accept all emotions.

l) Envision and feel yourself projecting love to the event. See its brightness, feel its warmth, know its beauty.

m) See God consciousness enveloping the event with love and appreciation.

n) Understand, at your very core, the place of this event in all of life and that you are part of divinity.

o) Give thanks to the event and take leave of it.

p) [Assume this is a WONDERFUL EVENT]. Remember forward to the event. Consider who you are and what you are like.

q) Invite the event into your space and ask that it connect with you.

r) Consider what wonderful things the event will bring to you.

s) Feel how you felt in the days after the wonderfulness: love, joy, fulfillment, health, inclusion, importance. Accept all emotions.

t) Envision and feel yourself projecting love to the event. See its brightness, feel its warmth, know its beauty.

u) See God consciousness enveloping the event with love and appreciation.

v) Understand, at your very core, the place of this event in all of life and that you are part of divinity.

w) Give thanks to the event and keep it in your awareness.

6. Give thanks and return from your Meditation slowly.

E. GRATITUDE MEDITATION

1. Find your place to Meditate. Your Meditation sweet spot or staged space.

2. Get comfortable and relax your body. Roll around on your hip bones, rotate your shoulders, move your fingers and toes, and find your comfort zone. Think of your body as a stick of butter, getting a gentle massage from the bottom of your feet up to the top of your head (don't forget your ears). As the massage moves up from one part of your body to the next, your body melts into nothing, like a warm stick of butter.

   Breathe in and out, focusing on your breath. Don't breathe harder, just a second or two longer. Equal breath in, hold equally, equal breath out.

3. Relax and quiet your mind. Let any thoughts gently pass by, without judgment or concern. Place persistent or particularly annoying thoughts into your Distraction Box.

   Breathe in and out, focusing on your breath. Don't breathe harder, just a second or two longer. Equal breath in, hold equally, equal breath out.

   Use your mantra if you wish. It can be as simple as counting from 1 - 10 and without breaking stride, continue counting from 1 - 10 again, in a loop. I use a slowly rotating water-wheel (in my mind) to help me stay on count.

4. Set an intention to find and expand gratitude in your life's experiences.

5. Consider 2 people or events that brought you great joy in your life and one future event that will be wonderful. We will focus on each one separately. It can be a parent, a sibling, a school mate, a teacher, a neighbor, a boss, etc. The person can be alive or dead. The event can be past, present, or future, although it is best to start with past events and work forward.

    a) [Assume this is a JOYFUL PERSON]. Visualize the person. Invite them into your space and ask that they connect with you.

    b) Consider what joy they brought you.

    c) Feel how you felt in the days after that experience: joy, love, and fulfillment. Accept all emotions.

    d) Envision and feel yourself projecting love to them. See its brightness, feel its warmth, know its beauty.

    e) See God consciousness enveloping the person with love and appreciation.

    f) Understand, at your very core, the love of this person and that they are divinity.

    g) Give thanks to the person and take leave of them.

h) [Assume this is another JOYFUL EVENT]. Remember back to the event. Consider who you were and what you were like.

i) Invite the event into your space and ask that it connect with you.

j) Consider what joy the event caused you.

k) Feel how you felt in the days after that experience: joy, love, and fulfillment. Accept all emotions.

l) Envision and feel yourself projecting love to the event. See its brightness, feel its warmth, know its beauty.

m) See God consciousness enveloping the event with love and appreciation.

n) Understand, at your very core, the place of this event in all of life and that you are part of divinity.

o) Give thanks to the event and take leave of them.

p) [Assume this is a FUTURE JOYFUL EVENT]. Remember forward to the event. Consider who you are and what you are like.

q) Invite the event into your space and ask that it connect with you.

r) Consider what wonderful things the event will bring to you.

s) Feel how you feel in the days after that joy: love, joy, fulfillment, health, inclusion, importance. Accept all emotions.

t) Envision and feel yourself projecting love to the event. See its brightness, feel its warmth, know its beauty.

u) See God consciousness enveloping the event with love and appreciation.

v) Understand, at your very core, the place of this event in all of life and that you are part of divinity.

w) Give thanks to the event and keep it in your awareness.

6. Give thanks and return from your Meditation slowly.

F. SELF-LOVE MEDITATION

1. <u>Find your place to Meditate.</u> Your Meditation sweet spot or staged space.

2. <u>Get comfortable and relax your body.</u> Roll around on your hip bones, rotate your shoulders, move your fingers and toes, and find your comfort zone. Think of your body as a stick of butter, getting a gentle massage from the bottom of your feet up to the top of your head (don't forget your ears). As the massage moves up from one part of your body to the next, your body melts into nothing, like a warm stick of butter.

   <u>Breathe in and out</u>, focusing on your breath. Don't breathe harder, just a second or two longer. Equal breath in, hold equally, equal breath out.

3. <u>Relax and quiet your mind.</u> Let any thoughts gently pass by, without judgment or concern. Place persistent or particularly annoying thoughts into your Distraction Box.

   <u>Breathe in and out</u>, focusing on your breath. Don't breathe harder, just a second or two longer. Equal breath in, hold equally, equal breath out.

   <u>Use your mantra if you wish.</u> It can be as simple as counting from 1 - 10 and without breaking stride, continue counting from 1 - 10 again, in a loop. I use a slowly rotating waterwheel (in my mind) to help me stay on count.

4. <u>Set an intention to find and expand self-love in your physical and energetic bodies.</u>

5. <u>Consider who you are.</u> Consider that God put you right where you are because he expresses his love *only* in very special ways.

    a) Visualize yourself. Visualize the joy and wonderment you have brought to others. Perhaps your parents, perhaps your siblings, perhaps your children, perhaps friends, strangers, and co-workers. Invite them into your space and ask that they connect with you.

    b) Love what you have brought to them.

    c) Appreciate how the special you was just what they needed in so many instances.

    d) Quietly absorb the love they feel for you. Visualize this love as God wrapping his arms around you and holding you firmly.

    e) Now see that his arms are your arms and your arms are his arms; know there is no separation between you, God, and others.

    f) Know now how it is that you came to be you in this time and place.

    g) Be still with that. It is perfection. It is pure. It is joy.

    h) People love you, people need you, people express to you, although that expression is not always recognized. You are a good person. Forgive yourself for your mistakes. Mistakes are part of growth.

Don't you think God could create people who could go through life without making mistakes if he wanted to? You're darn right he could. But if you don't learn, he doesn't grow, and he will never let a learning mistake really hurt you or someone else.

i) It hurts to make mistakes because it makes us feel imperfect, makes us feel like bad people. But we are not. Mistakes are simply part of life, no more, no less. Give them no emotion, definition, or rationale. Simply observe them and let them go away.

j) Love yourself for experiencing mistakes.

k) Visualize yourself. Visualize the joy and wonderment you have brought to God's creatures and plants and minerals. Do you remember feeling a puppy's excitement when it was playing with you? Do you remember how you became your cat's best friend every time you used the can opener? Did you ever gaze at a diamond, gem, or rock outcropping that left you without words. Have you ever stopped a busy day to admire a tree in the fall?

l) All these creatures, plants, and minerals are included in God's special way of sharing himself with you.

m) Love that sharing. Hold it as a precious gift.

n) Be still with that. It is perfection. It is pure. It is joy.

6. Give thanks and return from your Meditation slowly.

G. TRANSPARANCY MEDITATION (FOR HEALING AND HEALTH CARE PROFESSIONALS)

This Meditation is used to create a dialogue between yourself and someone with whom you have strong, usually negative, emotions. By understanding the other person's perspective, from *their* perspective, healing will occur.

This Meditation is very effective for: 1. Conflict Resolution; 2. Recovering from Trauma; and 3. Releasing Grief

1. <u>Find your place to Meditate.</u> Your Meditation sweet spot or staged space.

2. <u>Get comfortable and relax your body.</u> Think of your body as a stick of butter, getting a gentle massage from the bottom of your feet up to the top of your head (don't forget your ears). As the massage moves up from one part of your body to the next, your body melts into nothing, like a warm stick of butter.

   <u>Breathe in and out</u>, focusing on your breath. Don't breathe harder, just a second or two longer. Equal breath in, hold equally, equal breath out.

3. <u>Relax and quiet your mind.</u> Let any thoughts gently pass by, without judgment or concern. Place persistent or particularly annoying thoughts into your Distraction Box.

   <u>Breathe in and out</u>, focusing on your breath. Don't breathe harder, just a second or two longer. Equal breath in, hold equally, equal breath out.

Use your mantra if you wish. It can be as simple as counting from 1 to 10 and without breaking stride, continue counting from 1 to 10 again, in a loop. I use a slowly rotating water-wheel (in my mind) to help me stay on count.

4. Set an intention to find and experience compassion with the other person.

5. Consider that each person and creature is a special creation. Consider that each person and creature have taken different paths in life, most of them completely unseen by others. Be open to other perspectives and love them.

PART A – *You sharing concerns about another person with them, and then them responding back to you as you watch from their perspective.*

The purpose of Part A is for you to share concerns with another person with whom you have strong negative emotions around, and to hear back from them, from their perspective, as to why they did what they did. This will reduce the strong negative reactions in the relationship.

a) Visualize yourself sitting upright in a strong chair with a straight back. Knees together, feet flat on the floor. (You do not have to be in this position – but it helps).

b) Move your feelings and perspective into your being in your chair. Align your hips, legs, arms, hands, shoulders, feet, head, and eyes. Be you. Be Transparent with you. You are Person A.

c) Visualize an identical chair two to three feet in front of you, facing you.

d) Visualize the other person, Person B, sitting in that chair, them aligning into their body as you did yours.

e) Ask for loving guidance to emanate from this dialogue.

f) You, Person A, should say the following to Person B, addressing them by name.

    i. "_____, I wish to share with you things that make me _____ (angry, sad, resentful, mad, feel stupid, ...). I want you to know how I feel and what I think. The first thing is....."

    ii. State the three things you want the other person to know. (They can be two, it can be one, they can be more than three, but more than three tends to be a lot for most people).

    iii. EXAMPLE: "It really makes me feel stupid when you say I should 'get over it'. I am an intelligent adult and I will 'get over it', but the way I do that is to share how I feel about something with you. I need your support in helping me by simply listening to how I feel without trying to fix me."

    iv. State each concern concisely, clearly, without judgment or evaluation.

g) Move yourself into Person B's space in chair B just as you did with you in your space. Move your feelings and perspective into their being in their chair. Align your hips, legs, arms, hands, shoulders, feet, head, and eyes. Be that person. Be Transparent with that person. You are now Person B.

h) From your place inside Person B, view yourself in Person A. Emanate love from your heart in Person B into your heart in Person A.

i) Take a moment to do that, and then share a sentence or two with yourself, from Person B's perspective to you.

j) Address each of the concerns back to you from you inside Person B. Simply respond to your concerns without judgment or evaluation. Accept those responses and hold them quietly.

k) Move yourself back into you, Person A's space, just as you did a few minutes ago. Be Transparent with you. Move your feelings and perspective into your original being in chair A. Align your hips, legs, arms, hands, shoulders, feet, head, and eyes. Be that person. You are now back to being Person A.

l) Take a moment and consider what you have experienced, what you have learned. No judgment.

m) If you wish to share something back with Person B, please do so now. Appreciation and understanding tend to be most helpful. Apologies, if appropriate, can be stated, but understand that a lengthy apology is not necessary and can be unconstructive. Nature understands mistakes are part of life; hearing others with your heart is the truest way to express love.

n) Love yourself for experiencing mistakes.

PART B – The other person sharing things with you. This is OPTIONAL and can be omitted to keep the Meditation shorter. Part B's purpose is for Person A to learn something from Person B that they have not taken the time to hear, would allow to be spoken, or to hear from someone who has died or cannot be contacted.

If you skip Part B, move to Item 6.

The purpose of Part B is for you to hear from someone that you don't have interaction with or cannot have interaction with. It can be someone with whom you have friction or it can be someone that may simply have a different perspective of you. (Deep Dive students often use Part B to hear from themselves at an advanced age. For example, a student may wish to hear from themselves when they are age 85).

o) Visualize yourself sitting upright in a strong chair with a straight back. Knees together, feet flat on the floor. (You do not have to be in this position – but it helps).

p) Move your feelings and perspective into your being in the chair. Align your hips, legs, arms, hands, shoulders, feet, head, and eyes. Be that person. Be Transparent with that person. You are Person A.

q) Visualize an identical chair two to three feet in front of you, facing you.

r) Visualize the other person, Person B, sitting in that chair, them aligning into their body as you did yours.

s) Ask for loving guidance to emanate from this dialogue.

t) Now move into Person B's space, becoming Transparent with them, just as you have before.

u) Move your feelings and perspective into their being in their chair. Align your hips, legs, arms, hands, shoulders, feet, head, and eyes. Be that person. Be Transparent with that person. You are now Person B.

v) From your place inside Person B, look back at yourself in Chair A. Emanate love from your heart in Person B into your heart in Person A.

w) Take a moment to do that, and allow Person B to share two or three things with you, that they want you to know.

x) Take a moment and consider what you have heard, what has been shared with you. No judgment, no evaluation.

y) Move yourself back into you, Person A's space, just as you did a few minutes ago. Be Transparent with you. Move your feelings and perspective into your original being in Chair A. Align your hips, legs, arms, hands, shoulders, feet, head, and eyes. Be that person. Be Transparent with that person. You are now back to being Person A.

z) If you wish to share something back with Person B, please do so now. The point of Part B of this Meditation is for the other person to express to you things they wish to share; there is no need for you to respond although appreciation and love are always welcomed.

6. Give thanks and return from your Meditation slowly.

H. RETURN TO HEALTH FOR WOMEN - WEIGHT LOSS (AKA CHOCOLATE) MEDITATION

1. Find your place to Meditate. Your Meditation sweet spot or staged space.

2. Get comfortable and relax your body. Roll around on your hip bones, rotate your shoulders, move your fingers and toes, and find your comfort zone. Think of your body as a stick of butter, getting gentle massage from the bottom of your feet up to the top of your head (don't forget your ears). As the massage moves up from one part of your body to the next, your body melts into nothing, like a warm stick of butter.

   Breathe in and out, focusing on your breath. Don't breathe harder, just a second or two longer. Equal breath in, hold equally, equal breath out.

3. Relax and quiet your mind. Let any thoughts gently pass by, without judgment or concern. Place persistent or particularly annoying thoughts into your Distraction Box.

   Breathe in and out, focusing on your breath. Don't breathe harder, just a second or two longer. Equal breath in, hold equally, equal breath out.

   Use your mantra if you wish. It can be as simple as counting from 1 - 10 and without breaking stride, continue counting from 1 - 10 again, in a loop. I use a slowly rotating waterwheel (in my mind) to help me stay on count.

4. Set an intention to find and expand your understanding of true health and how it may manifest itself for you in your physical and energetic bodies.

5. Consider who you are and what you are made of. You are not your body and you are not your mind. You are something much greater and you contain great wisdom. You have been offered the chance to live inside your body while you walk upon the Earth. What gifts will you bestow to your Earthly Body?

   a) Sense where in your body where your main Consciousness and intelligence exist (it is generally not inside your head, but it could be). Your Body Intelligence is also your Body Essence, if you are using the Inner Essence Model.

   b) Feel your body before you came to it. Feel how it felt to itself. Was it excited? expressing joy? Or perhaps it was fearful, expressing anxiety?

   c) Feel what its expectations were for this life. Are those expectations the same today as they were then?

   d) No judgment. Just feel and appreciate them.

   e) Feel whether your body is housing judgment. If so, where is that judgment "holding up?" What is the shape of the judgment? Its size. Its density. Its color. Its temperature.

f) Share your feelings with this judgment that it is a normal self-protection mechanism, but now that your body is an adult body, it is no longer needed.

g) In your mind, look up and see a bright - but not blinding - light. Visualize and feel the judgment moving into the light to be taken forward where it next will be of great benefit.

h) Replace the area where this judgment used to be with a proper vision of self-worth. What is the shape of the new self-worth? Reflect on its size. Its density. Its color. Its temperature. Ask your Higher Guidance for a symbol to lock in the new self-worth and imprint it upon the new feeling.

i) Ask your Higher Guidance to share with you and your Body Consciousness / Body Essence what color your Body's improved health will be. See that color overlay and mesh with your Body Consciousness and physical Body.

j) Be with this for 8 minutes.

k) Know that improved health does not ever mean the loss of anything. Improved health comes naturally to you as you choose the nourishing food to share with your body. It comes naturally to you as you occasionally share joy with your body by tasting CHOCOLATES.

l) Know it comes naturally to you as you choose to share physical activity with your body.

m) Know it comes naturally to you as you offer your body nourishing sleep in darkened surroundings. Every now and then, share with your body the wonderful feeling of falling asleep after spending time under the stars of the night sky.

n) Know that improved health comes naturally to you as you share your body by immersion in Nature.

o) Be still with what you and your Body now understand. It is perfection. It is pure. It is joy.

6. Give thanks and return from your Meditation slowly.

I. INTRODUCTION TO YOUR INNER ESSENCES MEDITATION

You will see the Inner Essence graphic from Chapter 9 reproduced after this Meditation for reference.

1. Find your place to Meditate. Your Meditation sweet spot or staged space.

2. Get comfortable and relax your body. Roll around on your hip bones, rotate your shoulders, move your fingers and toes, and find your comfort zone. Think of your body as a stick of butter, getting a gentle massage from the bottom of your feet up to the top of your head (don't forget your ears). As the massage moves up from one part of your body to the next, your body melts into nothing, like a warm stick of butter.

    Breathe in and out, focusing on your breath. Don't breathe harder, just a second or two longer. Equal breath in, hold equally, equal breath out.

3. Relax and quiet your mind. Let any thoughts gently pass by, without judgment or concern. Place persistent or particularly annoying thoughts into your Distraction Box.

    Breathe in and out, focusing on your breath. Don't breathe harder, just a second or two longer. Equal breath in, hold equally, equal breath out.

    Use your mantra if you wish. It can be as simple as counting from 1 - 10 and without breaking stride, continue counting from 1 - 10 again, in a loop. I use a slowly rotating water-wheel (in my mind) to help me stay on count.

4. <u>Set an intention to discover and meet your Male or Female Inner Essence.</u>

5. Walk to Introduction. You are going to visualize a path that leads to a home, and inside that home you will meet your Inner Essence. If you are a female, have the intention to meet your Female Inner Essence, and if Male, have the intention to meet your male Inner Essence. If your intuition guides you to meet a different Inner Essence, please do so:

   a) Visualize yourself walking on the path. Feel with all five senses where you are. Are you in the woods, the dessert, along a beach, in the mountains, on an ice cap?. It does not matter which. Feel the temperature, the humidity, the sunlight or not, the time of day or night, the season.

   b) If nothing comes to you, CREATE IT in your mind and begin using all five senses. It does not matter if the scene comes to you own its own or if you create the scene. The results are exactly the same.

   c) As you walk along the path, feel the movement in your body. Is the path hard, soft, rocky, grassy, somewhere in between? Don't analyze—just softly notice. Move forward. Look around a bit and see what you see, hear what you hear, smell what you smell, taste what you taste.

   d) Continue to move purposefully.

e) Begin to notice that you are coming to a bend in the path. At the bend, the path opens into a clearing. Walk into that clearing.

f) Notice that there is a home off in the distance. Continue walking to the home.

g) Notice what the home looks like. Is it freshly painted? Is the yard neat and clean? Is it a wood structure, stone structure, glass structure, or something else?

h) You are getting near the house and are approaching the gate. Open the gate, close it behind you, and head to the door.

i) Step up onto the steps, approach the door and knock on it. Say in your mind and heart, "I wish to meet my Female Inner Essence or my Male Inner Essence; please come to the door."

j) The Inner Essence will open the door, and if he or she does not, open it yourself and enter. See your Inner Essence.

k) Ask your Inner Essence what name he or she wishes to be called. If you do not perceive an answer, simply gently ask again. Sometimes you may also get a symbol. If you still do not perceive a name, tell the Inner Essence you are going to call he or she "XXXX" until you are able to perceive their name.

l) If you do perceive the name, ask them why they wish to be called that name. Accept the answer and appreciate it. Have a dialogue around it if you wish.

m) Tell the Inner Essence what name you wish to be called and get their agreement on that.

n) Ask the Inner Essence how they are feeling. Explore the details of this. How a person or Inner Essence is feeling is usually so much more meaningful than what they are thinking.

o) If you find your Inner Essence has concerns, dialogue with them and determine a way to help them. It is appropriate for you to ask for something in return. Agree to specific actions, times, and outcomes, and stick to it.

p) Ask the Inner Essence if there is more they wish to share. Dialogue with them about that issue, if appropriate.

q) Give thanks to the Inner Essence. Tell them you will take leave of them now but will return. Invite them to communicate with you during your dreams. Thank them for their time and say good bye.

6. Give thanks and return from your Meditation slowly.

Inner Essences

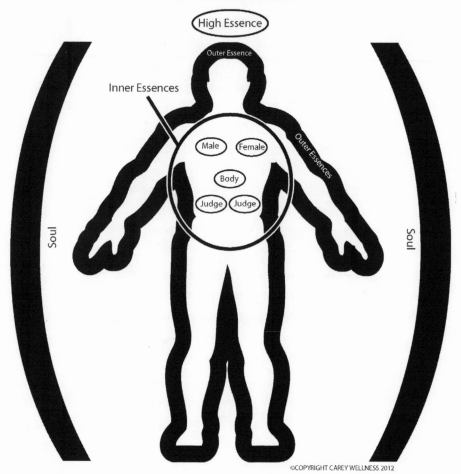

STRESS DOMINO CHART

CAREY WELLNESS STRESS DOMINO™

There are three conditions required for Stress to exist. If one or more of them is missing, you cannot be Stressed. In many instances, one may *appear* to be missing, but it is there, it is simply misunderstood.

The three conditions for STRESS to exist:

1. There is a THREAT to some aspect of you;
2. A FEAR must be activated in you; and
3. You perceive UNCERTAINTY (real or imagined).

There are three UNIVERSAL ILLUSIONS which are lies we tell ourselves. Most of these we first meet in childhood and then are reinforced later in life through jobs, politics, schools, religion, and advertising. Although these are not correct truths, but lies disguising themselves as truths, do not mistake their power and control over everyday life.

The three UNIVERSAL ILLUSIONS are:

1. You are absolutely ALONE and not connected to anybody or anything. You are separated from love;
2. There is a very limited amount of everything that exists; if you do not get it and get it now, there will not be enough left for you; and
3. You can be harmed or killed.

In using the Stress Domino you will learn to recognize these illusions for what they are (bullshit) and you will let them go. But life does not like a void so we will replace them with the three UNIVERSAL TRUTHS that the ILLUSIONS hide from you.

The three UNIVERSAL TRUTHS are:

1. All people and all things, particularly you, are connected to each other in a continuous stream of energy (LOVE);
2. There is more than enough for everybody, including you, regardless of how much or what specific things (including jobs) that other people have; and
3. You can never be harmed and you can never die. At some point your body may wear out or stop working due to disease or injury, yet your energetic you will always exist. Many people refer to the energetic you as your soul.

	CAREY Wellness Stress Domino™				
	Underlying Function	**A**	**B**	**C**	**Example**
1	Stress/ Stressful Situation	_____	_____	_____	<u>Rejection at asking someone out on a date</u>
2	Underlying Fear	_____	_____	_____	<u>I am not enough; people will laugh at me</u>
3	Three Universal Illusions	Match the FEAR in #2 with the underlying ILLUSION that supports it. Mark each that applies to each fear. There are sometimes more than one, rarely all three, and usually if there are 2 or more, one ILLUSION is dominant by a lot.			
	Illusion 1	_____	_____	_____	<u>Yes, mostly</u>
	Illusion 2	_____	_____	_____	<u>Yes, partially</u>
	Illusion 3	_____	_____	_____	<u>No</u>
4	Three Universal Truths	Match the ILLUSION above with the TRUTH the ILLUSION is hiding. As with ILLUSIONS, more than one may apply, but rarely three, and there is usually a dominant one.			
	Truth 1	_____	_____	_____	<u>Yes, mostly</u>
	Truth 2	_____	_____	_____	<u>Yes, partially</u>
	Truth 3	_____	_____	_____	<u>No</u>

Consider this: The TRUTHS in #4 are covered up by the ILLUSIONS in #3, which cause the FEARS in #2, which when ACTIVATED, cause the STRESS in #1.

When you replace the ILLUSIONS in #3 with the TRUTHS in #4, the Fears in #2 and the STRESSES in #1 will fall down around you, JUST LIKE DOMINOS!

Instructions to Completing the Table:

- Line1. Put in a STRESS in your life, a major one and/or one you've experienced recently. (A recent one can be a strong hint about what area to work on now.)

- Line 2. Feel and think about what the underlying FEAR may be. Write this here.

- Line 3. FEARS flow from misunderstandings which we call ILLUSIONS. Put an "X" next to the Illusion in Line 3 that causes the FEAR from Line 2.

- Line 4. The Universe does not like a vacuum. Put an "X" next to the TRUTH in Line 4 that best replaces the ILLUSION from Line 3.

To learn more about what Meditation can do for you and your Corporation, Organization, or Group ~ including for you personally and professionally ~ along with the investment required, please contact Chase Carey using the information below.

Chase Carey, MBA

Certified Meditation Teacher, Reiki Master, Jin Shin Jyutsu Practitioner, Personal Self Integration (Inner Essence) Teacher
O 770.751.6700
Info@CareyWellness
www.CareyWellness.com

Made in the USA
San Bernardino, CA
16 May 2014